GCSE
Questions and Answers

ENGLISH
KEY STAGE 4

Ian Barr Chief Examiner
Chris Walton Examiner

SERIES EDITOR: BOB McDUELL

Letts
EDUCATIONAL

Letts Educational
Aldine Place
London W12 8AW
Tel: 0181 740 2266
Fax: 0181 743 8451
e-mail: mail@lettsed.co.uk
website: http://www.lettsed.co.uk

First published 1995
Reprinted 1995 (twice), 1996
Revised 1996, 1997, 1998, 1999

Text: © Ian Barr and Chris Walton 1999

Design and illustrations: © BPP (Letts Educational) Ltd 1999

All our Rights Reserved. No part of this publication may be reproduced, stored in a retrieval system, or transmitted, in any form or by any means, electronic, mechanical, photocopying, recording or otherwise, without the prior permission of Letts Educational.

British Library Cataloguing in Publication Data
A CIP record for this book is available from the British Library.

ISBN 1 85758 953 X

Acknowledgements

Every effort has been made to trace copyright holders and to obtain their permission for the use of copyright material. The authors and publishers will gladly receive any information enabling them to rectify any error or omission in subsequent editions.

All answers are provided by the author. Permission for reproduction of questions from past papers has been granted by – or is pending from – the examination boards listed below. None of the boards has provided answers and none accepts responsibility for the answers suggested by the author. Answers provided may not necessarily constitute the only possible solutions.

Task 1 (p56): Reproduced by permission of the Northern Examination and Assessment Board. Task 3 (p59) and Task 3 (p62): Reproduced by permission of the Midland Examining Group. The Midland Examining Group and the University of Cambridge Local Examinations Syndicate bear no responsibility for the example answers to questions taken from their past question papers which are contained in this publication. Task 4 (p63): Reproduced by kind permission of London Examinations: A division of Edexcel Foundation (formerly ULEAC). Edexcel Foundation, London Examinations accepts no responsibility whatsoever for the accuracy or method of working in the answers given. Task 5 (p64): Reproduced by kind permission of the Southern Examining Group. Any answers or hints on answers are the sole responsibility of the author and have not been provided or approved by the Group. Task 6 (p66): Reproduced by kind permission of the Scottish Qualifications Authority (formerly SEB). Answers are the sole responsibility of the authors and have not been provided by the Board. Task 7 (p68) and 8 (p72): Reproduced by kind permission of the Welsh Joint Education Committee.

Article on p14 © Nicholas Roe, 1997. Article on p18 reproduced with permission from the May 1995 *Reader's Digest* magazine. Copyright © Reader's Digest Association May 1997. *The Hunchback in the Park* (p16) by Dylan Thomas, reprinted from *Collected Poems* published by JM Dent. *April Rise* (p16) by Laurie Lee, reprinted with permission of Peters Fraser and Dunlop Group Ltd. Advertisement (p20) reprinted with permission of Friends of the Earth. Extract on pp24–5 reproduced from *Pole to Pole* by Michael Palin with the permission of BBC Enterprises Limited. Article on pp38–39 reproduced with kind permission from an article by Brian Jenkins in *The Independent*, January 24 1994. Article on pp43–5 reproduced from the *AA magazine*, Issue 13, Summer 1995. Photographs on pp43–5 by Richard Newton. Illustration on p44 by Tim Slade. Poem on p56 reproduced from *Standing Female Nude* by Carol Ann Duffy, published in 1995 by Anvil Press Poetry Ltd. Extract on pp57–9 reproduced from *American Short Stories of Today* published by Penguin, and originally in an anthology published by Faber and Faber. Article on pp59–61 adapted and reproduced from an article by Peter Silverton, © the Observer. Photograph on p62 by Nils Jorgensen © Rex Features Ltd. Extract on pp64–5 from *The Pupil* by Caro Fraser published by Phoenix. Photograph on p66 reproduced by permission of BUPA. Extract on pp67–8 reproduced from *The Ghost Road* by Pat Barker (Viking 1995) © Pat Barker 1995, reproduced by permission of Penguin Books Ltd. Extract on pp70 © Bill Bryson 1995, extracted from *Notes from a Small Island* by Bill Bryson, published by Black Swan, a division of Transworld Publishers Ltd. All rights reserved. Flyer on pp 71 & 72 © Conwy County Council, reproduced by kind permission. Article on p79 © Telegraph Group Limited, London, 1997.

Prepared by *specialist* publishing services, Milton Keynes

Printed in Great Britain by Ashford Colour Press

Letts Educational is the trading name of BPP (Letts Educational) Ltd

Contents

HOW TO USE THIS BOOK	1
ASSESSMENT OBJECTIVES IN ENGLISH	2
EXAMINATION TECHNIQUE	3

1 REVISION SUMMARIES — 4

2 DIFFERENT WRITING TASKS
- Writing to inform, explain and describe — 14
- Writing to explore, imagine and entertain — 16
- Writing to analyse, review and comment — 18
- Writing to argue, persuade and instruct — 20
- A particular skill – writing a summary — 22

3 RESPONDING TO DIFFERENT KINDS OF STIMULUS MATERIAL
- Comprehension — 24
- Pre-twentieth century literary stimulus — 31
- Twentieth century literary stimulus — 33
- Media stimulus — 38
- Non-fiction stimulus — 43
- Media and non-fiction stimuli — 48

4 SPEAKING AND LISTENING — 54

5 EXAM PRACTICE
- Tasks — 56
- Examiner's tips — 73
- Mock examination paper — 77

Introduction

HOW TO USE THIS BOOK

Although this book has been fairly substantially revised for 1999, its aim remains to provide you, the student, with the help you need to reach the highest level of achievement possible in one of your most important examinations – the General Certificate of Secondary Education (GCSE) or, in Scotland, at General and Credit levels. The book is designed to help all students, up to and including A* grade at GCSE.

Undoubtedly, you will know that syllabuses have been revised substantially for 1999 and the authors have checked changes in the style of questioning associated with the revised syllabuses. We continue in our belief that experienced examiners can provide, through examination questions, sample answers and advice, the help a student needs to ensure success.

The primary consideration has been to present the main principles on which study can be based so that confidence can grow as weaknesses are identified and eliminated.

The *Questions and Answers* series is designed to provide:

- easy-to-use **revision summaries** which identify important information that the student must understand if progress is to be made answering examination questions. Spend some time on this section first and refer back to it whenever you find it necessary. There should not be anything in this section which is brand new; you will find that you have covered all the things referred to in class, but it will be useful to remind yourself of all the things covered in this section.

- advice on the **different types of task** (or question) and how to answer them well to obtain the highest marks. We have included in the book a range of different types of task using **different types of stimulus material**. In one sense the technique you should use is always the same – read the stimulus material carefully, make notes, think and then complete the task taking care to revise your first attempt. However, associated with each task, or set of tasks, are specific notes which should help you both in approaching what you have to do and in reviewing what you have done.

- information about other skills which will be tested on examination papers apart from the recall of knowledge. These are sometimes called **assessment objectives**. Modern GCSE examinations put great emphasis on the testing of objectives other than knowledge and understanding. Assessment objectives include communication, problem solving, evaluation and interpretation.

- many examples of **examination questions**. A student can improve by studying a sufficiently wide range of questions providing they are shown the way to improve their answers to these questions. Some of the questions come from actual examination papers or specimen materials published by examination boards. Other questions have been written by examiners and aim to mirror closely real examination questions set by examination boards. The questions meet the requirements of all British examination boards.

- **sample answers** to some of the questions. They are not perfect answers but they point the way forward for you and perhaps they challenge you to do better. We would suggest that you might consider having a go at some of the tasks before reading the sample answers and then comparing what you have written with the sample answer. Without doubt this will give you food for thought. Remember, though, that there are rarely right or wrong answers in English.

- **advice from examiners**. By using the experience of actual examiners we are able to give advice which can enable the student to see how their answers can be improved and success be ensured.

Introduction

ASSESSMENT OBJECTIVES IN ENGLISH

Assessment objectives are linked very closely with the **attainment targets** of the National Curriculum and it is easiest to look at them in detail by linking them with those attainment targets.

Objective 1: Speaking and Listening

- You must be able to demonstrate that you can speak about personal experiences and be able to express your views and feelings.
- You must be able to discuss things in a group and show that you can express your own views and also listen to the views of others.
- You must be able to explain things clearly.
- You must be able to demonstrate that you can work with a group to make a presentation.
- You must be able to show that you understand that how you speak may well change according to your audience and your intentions.
- You must use standard English, which means grammatically correct English.
- You must demonstrate that you can listen carefully and sympathetically to other speakers.

Objective 2: Reading

- You must be able to demonstrate that you have read a wide range of books with insight and engagement. In your writing you must be able to make appropriate references to the texts and you must be able to sustain interpretations of them.
- You must show that you have read material from the media, newspapers and magazines and also material from non-fiction which might include, for instance, travel books and biographies.
- You must be able to show that you can follow an argument, that you can distinguish between fact and opinion and that you understand why things are written in a particular way.
- You must be able to extract information from different texts and use that information.
- You must be able to judge how writers use language to achieve their effects and you must be able to comment on the language.

Objective 3: Writing

- You must show that you can write in different ways for different purposes and can plan your writing, by writing in paragraphs and using correct punctuation.
- You must be able to show that you can use a range of suitable vocabulary.
- You must show that you know how to revise, edit and improve your writing.
- You must be able to use the grammatical structures of standard English and a wide vocabulary to express your meanings precisely and clearly.

The *Questions and Answers* series helps you to develop skills and your abilities to meet these assessment objectives by the use of questions and by examining possible answers and commenting on them. You might refer to the assessment objectives to help you answer the basic question, "What am I required to do?"

Introduction

EXAMINATION TECHNIQUE

Success in GCSE examinations comes from proper preparation and a positive attitude to the examination. This book is intended to help you overcome "examination nerves" which often come from a fear of not being properly prepared. Examination technique is extremely important and certainly affects your performance. Remember the basics:

- Read the questions carefully.
- Make sure that you watch the time carefully and complete the paper. It is no good answering one question well if you spend so long doing it that you do not answer another question at all.
- Make sure that you answer the right number of questions. Read the rubric on the front of the examination paper carefully and keep it in mind.
- Examination papers usually tell you how many marks are available for each answer. Take notice of this information as the number of marks gives a guide to the importance of the question and often to the amount which you ought to write.
- Remember to leave time to check through your work carefully.

  Use this book for practice and to gain confidence. Good luck!

Revision summaries

English is not the same as maths and science. It is not as if you can revise all that you have learnt in the hope that the topics will appear in questions on the exam paper.

However, you can so easily throw marks away in English exams by being careless or slovenly. The idea of these revision summaries is to help you eliminate all those silly errors. The aim is to help you to become accurate. Use the summaries to remind you of some of the approaches you need to perform well in written tasks, and of some of the technical points in the composition of writing, but remember that you will only be accurate if you make an effort to get things right in your own work.

SPELLING

You are not allowed to take a dictionary or spell-check into the examinations, but you should use them when you are doing your coursework.

You cannot be expected to spell every word in the English language correctly. However, regular use of a dictionary during your course will help you to master spelling.

Half the battle with accurate spelling is to avoid **careless** errors. To put this point another way, it is important that **you should want to get spellings right!** Be aware of careless errors; check over your work; always be thinking about spellings. At the very least this may help you to cut down the number of errors you make.

There are some very basic spellings which cause confusion. Sometimes they are spellings of words which sound similar but in fact mean something very different. Here are some examples of words which are often confused and misspelt:

there, they're, their,

wear, we're, were, where,

no, know, now,

it's, its,

how, who,

whose, who's.

You are going to create a very poor impression if you make these simple errors. Make sure you have learnt the differences. Here are examples to help you learn them:

There are important exams next week. The pupils taking the exams hope **they're** going to pass.

They have been told that they will get **their** results in the summer.

Cricketers **wear** whites for the match.

The commentator said, "Let's hope **we're** in for a good match!"

Where is the match being played?

Everybody will **know** about the party. There will be **no** food left over.

Now the music can start.

It's nearly time for the holidays.

The school finished **its** term early. (Some hopes!)

How easy is it to play tennis? There are some people **who** will say that it is very easy.

It was difficult to decide **whose** service was better.

I am sure that she is the player **who's** going to win.

Write out another example for each of these simple words, in order to make sure that you can get them right.

Revision summaries

VOCABULARY

To move towards the higher grades in English you need to be able to use an appropriate and extensive vocabulary. You also need to be able to write in the form of standard English, which will affect your choice of vocabulary. This section is presented as some questions and answers to help you think about vocabulary.

What can I do to develop my vocabulary in a piece of writing?
Always be thinking of alternatives. Never just accept the first word that comes to mind. Never use words sloppily, or words which do not mean much (e.g. "get" or "nice").

What is meant by "appropriate" vocabulary?
This means choosing the right tone of word. For a report or a formal letter you should not use colloquialisms or slang ("well good" or "wicked"). Indeed in this kind of writing you should try to be as precise as possible. In a more imaginative piece, however, you might well choose to use colloquialisms or slang for effect.

What else can I do to achieve an appropriate vocabulary?
Try to vary your use of words and avoid repetition, especially in the same sentence or paragraph. Remember that by using adjectives (words which describe nouns) and adverbs (words which describe verbs, usually ending in -ly), you can add to the precision of your writing.

How can I extend my vocabulary?
By becoming more interested in the meanings of words, usually through wide reading. Make sure you regularly read the newspaper, especially in the period approaching your exam. You may have a lot of work to do, but continue reading books for pleasure too, right up to the last minute before your exam. As you do so you will continue to take in vocabulary.

Now for a word or two about **clichés**. A cliché is an overworked phrase or word. It is the sort of thing which has been said or written hundreds of times before, and, as a result, when you use it it does not mean anything. Stories sometimes start with "It was a bright summer day…". Can you see why this is a cliché? Or, "The clouds looked like cotton wool…".

How can I avoid clichés in my writing?
This will depend on the kind of writing that you are doing. If it is an imaginative piece, try to picture precisely what you are describing. Always try to visualise your events or scenes. If it is an informative piece, try to be clear precisely what you are arguing or stating. On paper, in rough, or in your head, go over the points you are making before you write them down. This should give you a better chance of choosing the most appropriate words.

Should I try to learn new words?
Well, there is no point in forcing out words on to the page if they are just there for effect! That can appear silly. There is a lot to be said for using a thesaurus, however, especially when doing coursework. Above all, a thesaurus can make you enthusiastic for new words.

PARAGRAPHING

When you write you need to use paragraphs for TWO main reasons:
1. your ideas must be organised;
2. you will make it easier for the reader to follow what you are writing (how important is this in an exam?!)

What is a paragraph?
A paragraph is a section of writing. Writers stop after they have covered a point, or a series of related points, and at a suitable moment, start a new section. When we write in handwriting, which we always do in an exam, we **indent** the start of our new paragraphs. (You will find that this

Revision summaries

happens in books although increasingly writers using word processors do not indent in all documents.) **YOU MUST INDENT!!** However, there is an exception: there is no need to indent the **first paragraph** of a story or essay.

What do we mean by indent? Look at where I positioned the "w" in the first word of this sentence. What do you notice about it? It is slightly moved in from the margin. If you find it difficult to remember to do this, you could also leave a line between one paragraph and the next. You will find helpful examples of the layout of paragraphs in the extracts from the "stimulus material" and "exam practice" sections of this book. Have a good look at these and make sure you understand how paragraphs are set out.

What do you need to do to make sure that you are using paragraphs?

❶ Use your plan. You do not necessarily need to number each paragraph but it helps if you have been able to **jot down your points in a sequence** which can then form each paragraph. Keep looking back at your plan as this can provide you with a guide for your paragraphs.

❷ As you are writing, think about the **organisation of ideas, events, descriptions, arguments, key points etc.** OK, so it is difficult! A lot of pupils say that they forget to use paragraphs because they are lost in thought. They are too tied up with the ideas in their writing. So try to look up every now and again. **Step back from the page and ask yourself questions about the layout of your work.** You may find it helpful to think of it like painting a picture. If your eye is too close to the canvas, you cannot see the whole picture. You need to look at the arrangement of objects in the work, as well as the detail.

How many paragraphs?

There are no easy answers to this question. If you have too many paragraphs and they are then too short, it will suggest that your ideas are too shallow, too simple. On the other hand, overlong paragraphs will make you guilty of inadequate organisation. **You must strike a balance!** One area where you need regular paragraphing is when you are reporting speech in a story. For revision of this see the following revision summary on punctuation.

PUNCTUATION

When you write you need to use punctuation for THREE main reasons:

❶ you can show the relationships between one part of a sentence and another;

❷ you can help to stress emphasis or tone in what you are writing;

❸ you will be able to organise your work.

What punctuation do you need to be able to use?

FULL STOPS: to mark the ends of sentences. But do not break down your writing into sentences which are too short. That's too easy.

COMMAS: for a variety of reasons, such as to mark off one clause from the remainder of the sentence, to establish a pause, to give one word or a few words special emphasis.

CONFUSION BETWEEN FULL STOPS AND COMMAS: sometimes it is easy to confuse the use of commas and full stops. As a general rule any sentence should contain **only one MAIN verb**. If you realise that you are about to start a new "unit of sense", then use a full stop and start a new sentence. Never use a comma loosely when you are really starting a new sentence. However, try to combine or merge sentences to make them more complex – for this you will need the comma regularly.

COLONS AND SEMI-COLONS: Colons (:) are used to introduce lists or to introduce main points of discussion and argument. There are many examples of colons on this page. **Semi-colons** (;) are used to join together two sentences that are very close in their meanings or as a replacement for commas when separating points in a list.

Revision summaries

QUESTION MARKS AND EXCLAMATION MARKS: Question marks (?) always end a sentence which asks a question. Note that a question mark contains its own full stop and does not require another one. **Exclamation marks** (!) should be used at the end of a sentence which expresses something very strongly or humorously. But use them sparingly. Too many of them can ruin the effect for the reader.

SPEECH MARKS: also known as **inverted commas** or **quotation marks**, they exist to punctuate **direct** or **reported speech** and also for **titles** and **quotations**. There are some basic guidelines: place the marks at the start and finish of all the speech, including all other marks of punctuation; following the words spoken, when you return to the narrative, continue the sentence – do not use capital letters; if you are reporting the speech of more than one speaker follow the rules of paragraphing, starting each new speaker on a new line and indenting the first words. Remember what was said about paragraphing on pages 5–6.

HYPHENS: for joining words or parts of words; **DASHES:** for separating words or phrases for a particular effect; **BRACKETS:** for marking off phrases or words which are additional to the main sentence (often asides, clarifications, alternatives etc.); **APOSTROPHES:** see the following section.

APOSTROPHES

There are TWO types of apostrophe:
1. the apostrophe of omission;
2. the apostrophe of possession.

THE APOSTROPHE OF OMISSION: for use when you are writing a word or combination of words which have been **contracted** and you have left out a letter or more than one letter. This should not be difficult to understand. Simply replace the letter or letters that have been left out with an apostrophe (').

Here are some common contractions in everyday use: it's… he's… we'll… don't… can't.
In each of the above words, which letters have been omitted?
There is another type of omission. This is when you are reporting the way characters speak in a realistic way and you wish to represent accent or dialect.

E.g. 'e's really bin workin' 'ard to pass 'is exams!

THE APOSTROPHE OF POSSESSION (OR POSSESSIVE APOSTROPHE): for use when, in the grammar of your sentence, something belongs to another word, or is literally possessed by another word. This apostrophe is usually called the **apostrophe s**. There are differences between where you place the **apostrophe s** according to whether you have a singular noun "owner" or a plural noun "owner". There is a simple way of remembering the difference. Singular nouns have **'s** and plural nouns have **s'** at the end of the word. Study the difference in the examples below:

For **singular** nouns: The **pupil's** books. (There is only one pupil.)
The **girl's** pen. (There is only one girl.)

For **plural** nouns: The **athletes'** times. (There is more than one athlete.)
The **boys'** games. (There is more than one boy.)

For **plural nouns which do not end in "s"**: The **women's** coats
The **gentlemen's** outfitter.

One word which always causes confusion: its – when you use the word **its** as a possessive pronoun, it does not require a possessive apostrophe. Neither do **his, her, their, our**… so do not be tempted to use one with **its**.

E.g. The dog returns to **its** bone.
The tree sheds **its** leaves.

See above, in the section on the apostrophe of omission, for the use of the word **it's**.

1 Revision summaries

SPEECH MARKS

1 When the speech comes first:
"There was a huge fire in our road last night," said the worried child.

What to look out for: all the words spoken are contained within the inverted commas; the punctuation (comma) is also contained within the inverted commas; no need for a capital letter after the reported speech – the word "said" simply continues the sentence; the start of the line (paragraph) is indented.

2 When the speech comes second:
The worried child said, "There was a huge fire in our road last night."

What to look out for: again, all the words spoken are contained within the inverted commas; the full stop at the end is contained within the inverted commas; a comma is used to separate the story from the speech (what else could you have used here, instead of a comma?); the start of the line (paragraph) is indented.

3 Mostly speech, a bit of narrative in between:
"There was a huge fire in our road last night," said the worried child, "and there were lots of fire engines!"

4 Other combinations of speech and narrative:
"There was a huge fire in our road last night," said the worried child, "and there were lots of fire engines! You could see the flames right up in the sky." Then she suddenly seemed to remember something important: "but nobody was hurt," she added.

5 When you have more than one speaker:
"There was a huge fire in our road last night," said the worried child, "and there were lots of fire engines!"

"What caused it?" asked his friends.

"I don't know. There are rumours about arson," he replied.

What to look out for: most importantly, notice that each new speaker is given a new line, indented, as each new line is a new paragraph.

Which to use, single (' ') or double (" ") inverted commas?
It is entirely up to you. But remember, whichever you choose, be consistent throughout a piece of work. You cannot vary between single and double – that would be very poor style.

USEFUL TERMS

There are a number of technical terms about language which are helpful in both reading and writing. In responses to reading – comprehensions, appreciations of literature, etc. you may need to use some of the terms, and they may also help you with your own writing. This list includes the basic **parts of speech**.

You will also be aware that you are marked in some sections of your exams for **knowledge about language**. This sometimes involves the use of technical terms to identify and describe features of language. The terms are listed alphabetically here:

Accent: a regional manner of pronunciation.

Acronym: an abbreviation, often instantly recognisable, usually formed from a combination of the first letters of a group of words. Sometimes acronyms are pronounced by their letters (AA, GCSE, RE, the UN, the USA, etc.), sometimes by a word that becomes formed by the first letters of the sequence of words (NATO), and sometimes by a combination of letters (OXFAM).

Adjective: a word used to describe or qualify a noun. Adjectives can express various features, e.g. quality (*big, small, rough, smooth*), quantity (*many, six*), distinguishing features (a *terraced* house, as opposed to a *detached* house).

Revision summaries

Adverb: a word used to describe or qualify a verb. Adverbs often end in the letters *ly*. (He ran *quickly*, she walked *briskly*) – but there are many exceptions (He moved *sideways*, she ran *forward*, they were *often* late). Adverbs also serve the purpose of qualifying adjectives (He was *definitely* late, she was *beautifully* tanned), and other adverbs (She ran *extremely* quickly, he walked *very* slowly).

Alliteration: when sounds are repeated deliberately, usually in the lines of a poem, to create an effect (*When **w**eeds, in **w**heels, shoot **l**ong and **l**ovely and **l**ush* – "Spring", by Gerard Manley Hopkins).

Ambiguity: double meanings – often writers deliberately want to suggest or imply more than one meaning in a phrase or word (*see also* irony).

Analogy: a comparison which does not use imagery. Writers often describe a situation or event which is comparable to another one, the effect being that we can then understand the second situation more clearly (e.g. a story about tragic young love might be *analogous* to the story of *Romeo and Juliet*).

Argument essay: writing which presents points of view or opinion, usually backed up by facts and evidence.

Assonance: a combination of vowel sounds, commonly used in poetry, in order to add effect (*The morning-dream that hover'd o'er her head* – "The Rape of the Lock", by Alexander Pope, l. 22).

Attitude: the outlook or point of view held by a writer.

Audience: now a commonly used term to mean "reader". Writers with a clear sense of audience are able to ask the key questions: who am I writing for and for what purpose? They will then be able to use the most appropriate style, tone or register. The term is particularly useful if you are writing for a clear group of readers, e.g. a story for young children, a set of rules for school, a letter to the newspaper to complain about an issue. But it is not always a useful term – sometimes we just write for ourselves, or for a very general purpose, with no particular audience in mind.

Ballad: a poem that tells a story. Ballads often rhyme and are frequently associated with traditional stories, sometimes based on legend, often derived from old folk tales with romantic, supernatural or other atmospheric settings.

Blank verse: unrhymed poetry.

Characterisation: how a writer will use language to build up and reveal characters (e.g. through speech, description of appearance, actions, etc.).

Clause: a distinct part of a sentence – as opposed to *phrases*, which are often just a few words. Clauses form units of meaning, like a sentence within a sentence, always with one main verb.

Cliché: a tired, habitually overworked phrase (see p5 for examples).

Colloquialisms: words or phrases which are informal, familiar, part of everyday speech, rather than appropriate in formal styles of writing – try to avoid colloquialisms in more formal writing, but you can use them to good effect, providing they fit the style, in more imaginative pieces.

Conjunction: a joining or linking word in a sentence (*and, or, but, because, if, though*, etc.).

Connotation: a suggested or implied meaning which a word carries with it. Names of animals often hold connotations (pig, fish, snake, etc.), that is, the words have come to hold associations for us other than just as animals.

Derivation: the origins of words.

1 Revision summaries

Description: language used to create a picture of places, people, objects, moods, etc. Some might say that all parts of literature are, by their nature, descriptive, but some passages are brought more vividly to life by a writer's careful use of detail.

Dialect: local variation of standard English.

Dialogue: two or more characters speaking with each other. Note also how important speech is in literature to create characters.

Diction: the choice of words to give a particular slant to meanings – consider, for example, the differences suggested by these words: pupil/student; spectator/fan; storm/tempest.

Direct speech: speech reported in writing (see p8).

Drafting: the process of writing, from the early stages through to refining ideas and then final copy, including proof-reading and editing.

Empathy: the ability of a writer to relate to an experience outside their own – to get into somebody else's mind or experiences. This is a skill commonly required in your writing at GCSE – frequently you are asked to take on the role of a particular character.

Evocation (evoke/evocative): the capacity of a writer to bring to life certain memories, feelings, associations – sometimes to call up a certain mood or atmosphere, or a sense of place.

Figurative language: non-literal use of language, often in the form of imagery, but sometimes as figures of speech, e.g. in sayings or proverbs (*a bird in the hand is worth two in the bush* or *out of the frying pan, into the fire*).

Formal and **informal registers:** a formal register of language will be marked out by complete sentences, precise vocabulary, complex grammar, and an informal register might use colloquialisms, slang, shortened sentences, in writing which will seem more like conversation.

Genre: a type or collection of writing, e.g. romantic, realistic, Gothic, a fable, a ballad, a satire – the key thing is that to belong to a genre, a work will contain certain distinguishing features marking it out as a particular type of writing.

Grammar: the construction of language.

Hero: the principal character in a novel or play. Usually, to be a hero we expect the main character to be a decent sort of character, one who can be admired or held in high esteem.

Homophone: words which sound the same, but which have different meanings and perhaps different spellings, for example *knight* and *night*.

Hyperbole: exaggeration. To coin a modern phrase, this is when writers "go over the top" with their use of language, suggesting that something is the strongest, the best, the greatest, which of course usually distorts the truth (here is another example from "The Rape of the Lock": *Belinda smiled, and all the world was gay.*).

Idiom: a phrase or expression in current use. Often like colloquialisms, these will be familiar, or conversational, or even figurative (*nice weather for the ducks* or *she gave me a piece of her mind*).

Revision summaries

Imagery: a non-literal contrast. There are three common types of images used (examples are again taken from "The Rape of the Lock"):

Similes: *her eyes*
like the sun, shine on all alike

(a simile makes a comparison by stating that one thing is like another).

Metaphors: in another part of the poem, the writer refers to a pair of scissors:

The little engine on his fingers ends …

(a metaphor allows the object simply to become what it is being compared with, so in this case the scissors become the little engine, and there is no need for the writer to state that they are like the engine – in this way a metaphor is a more direct comparison).

Personification: this involves turning an object – either inanimate or from nature – into a human or animal form, with human or animal actions and feelings. Pope is here writing about the River Thames:

Thames with pride surveys his rising towers.

It is essential to understand what is meant by *non-literal* language: eyes cannot literally be the sun; a pair of scissors cannot literally be an engine; a river cannot literally survey towers with pride!

Intonation: stress placed on different words, syllables, etc.; used to emphasise key points and often termed the "punctuation of speech".

Irony: saying, or writing, one thing, and meaning another. Think of it as a form of sarcasm. For example, we might say "well done" to make fun of a friend who trips over some steps. Irony in literature is much the same, and is quite often intended to make fun of characters, reveal their weaknesses or to mock them. So, to find ironic language, look for hidden or double meanings.

Jargon: a sort of vocabulary known mostly to particular groups, e.g. of workers; "buzzwords" or an "in-language", maybe used exclusively.

Mockery: speech used ironically, perhaps sarcastically, to create humour.

Monologue: the opposite of dialogue – a character speaking aloud to him or herself.

Mood: often used nowadays to mean tone or atmosphere. You may be asked to describe the mood of some writing: is it sad, tragic, positive, optimistic, romantic, or some other mood? Often you can see how mood has been created by analysing the use of adjectives and adverbs.

Narrator: the teller of a story; we often talk of "**the narrator's voice**". Who is telling the story? Does the teller of the story play a part in it? Is it written in the **first person**, or the **third person**, by the **omniscient narrator**? All of this makes up **narrative technique** – the ways in which a story is written.

Noun: that part of speech which is object (*knife*), thing (*gas*), place (*city*), abstraction (*happiness*), state (*death*), event (*game*), person (*mother*). **Proper nouns** are names or titles (*The Cup Final, John, London*, etc.).

Onomatopoeia: a word used to suggest its meaning by its sound, such as *crash* or *scream*, although clearly, in poetry, the effect will be less obvious, as in this, another example from "The Rape of the Lock": *Now lap-dogs give themselves the rousing shake.* (l.15)

Plot: the plan of events in a story or play – effectively the plot is what happens, as opposed to the subject or themes.

1 Revision summaries

Pronoun: words such as *I, you, he, she, we, they, which, whose* – all words which replace nouns (or more accurately, which replace noun phrases).

Prose: the best way to define prose is to think of it as that writing which is *not* poetry. It is most commonly the writing in stories and novels, and will be characterised by the use of continuous sentences and paragraphs, but it is difficult to give a precise definition.

Pun: a play on words, involving double meanings, sometimes using homophones – words that sound the same, but with different meanings and perhaps different spellings. Shakespeare used a lot of these sorts of puns. *Julius Caesar* begins with a famous one: A citizen of Rome is asked what his job is, and he, a cobbler, jokingly replies that he is a "mender of bad *soles*" – can you see the pun, or double meaning, suggested by the sound of the word?

A lot of modern newspaper headlines are full of puns, often where there is an association of meanings between words: FAMOUS CRICKETER GIVEN BAIL ... POLICEMAN JOINS BEAT GROUP ... VICAR IS PREY OF LOCAL THUGS ... think of your own!

Realism: writing which shows life as it really is – frequently writing which captures a sense of the truth, almost like a photograph or descriptive painting. The effect is often created by mention of down-to-earth objects, recognisable features, or dialogue which can almost be heard as if spoken aloud.

Register: an increasingly common term, used to mean the type of language being used in any particular situation; perhaps the best way to define register is by the word *variety* – possible different registers are: literary, poetic, formal, informal, presentational, gossip, argumentative, lecture, discursive, informative, persuasive ... but really the list is endless.

Rhetoric: nowadays we tend to use this term to mean persuasive, frequently elegant language, used in speeches and argument. Sometimes it is used as a way of criticising a speaker by implying that he has used words powerfully and convincingly, but without much substance in the argument. In the past, rhetoric more accurately meant "the art of speech-making".

Rhyme: words placed in a relationship in poetry, frequently at the ends of lines, due to their sounding the same, e.g.

> Behold, four kings in majesty *revered*,
> With hoary whiskers and a forky *beard*.   "The Rape of the Lock", l. 37–8.

Rhythm: the metre, or the beat, of lines in poetry.

Satire: mockery, intended to poke fun at characters in order to expose their weaknesses, their foolishness, or their immorality. A good way to think of satire is to think of the popular television programme, *Spitting Image*.

Slang: alternative words used by groups of people, often all from the same area.

Standard English: the form of written and spoken English generally agreed as most appropriate for use in public contexts, e.g. work, formal communications, business, education, journalism, etc.

Soliloquy: a speech in a play spoken by one character to the audience only – really a character thinking aloud; a technique used a great deal by Shakespeare.

Style: that part of literature which is to do with the expression, as opposed to the content, ideas, themes or subject matter – style is always associated with *how* literature is written rather than *what* it is about.

Revision summaries

Symbol: the use of one thing to represent or suggest something else, in literature. We talk about objects or events being symbolic of a mood, feeling or idea, even if at first glance they do not appear related.

Syntax: the way that sentences are constructed.

Themes: connected ideas which arise in literature, often revealed through the actions of more than one character, a number of events, or with features of the language which are expressed more than once. For example, we might discover themes of love, fate, power, despair, innocence, evil, all to be interpreted from different parts of a work of literature. Some of the main themes in Shakespeare's plays would be impatience in *Romeo and Juliet*; mischief in *A Midsummer Night's Dream*; honour in *Julius Caesar*.

Tone: the overall mood or feeling of language. For example, the tone could be humorous, tragic, persuasive, sympathetic, mocking, serious, etc.

Verb: many young children are taught that verbs are "doing words", but this definition is now rejected as inadequate; more strictly, a verb is a "happening" or "occurring" word – the word(s) needed for something to take place in a sentence. Sentences cannot be formed without verbs, they would end up making no sense, as would be the case in the following example:

> The athlete *won* the race.
>
> Remove the verb, and see what you are left with:
>
> The athlete the race.

Vocabulary: the variety and selection of words. It is an important skill to extend your vocabulary, and the best way to do so is by using a thesaurus.

Voice: now a common term used to mean "the writer's sense of presence in a piece of writing". You have probably been told by your teachers to "put something of yourself into your writing" – this is achieved by being interested in what you have to say, so that there is evidence that you as a writer are genuinely expressing yourself.

2 Different writing tasks

This section aims to remind you of the range of **types of writing** that you need to be able to do in English exams. Writing is a very varied sort of activity. You need to be able to distinguish between the different demands of writing imaginatively, writing formally, writing to inform or to describe, writing personally, and writing for a particular audience.

There is also reference to **reading** and **understanding** skills in this section. It is, after all, very rarely that we write without involving ourselves in reading, and responding to what we read. Try not to separate reading and writing in your mind. Think of one as dependent on the other.

WRITING TO INFORM, EXPLAIN AND DESCRIBE

One type of writing which you are required to do, no matter which syllabus you are studying, is writing to inform, explain or describe.

Here is a newspaper article about an aspect of the health of school pupils. Read the article to give you ideas and then complete the task which follows.

STIMULUS MATERIAL

The schoolbag fashion victims

Schoolchildren are carrying bags as 'a style statement' but, says Nicholas Roe, their long-term health could suffer.

POPPY, Charlotte and Tamsin are sitting round a table discussing the most important fashion accessory in the teen wardrobe. "It shows what kind of person you are," they insist. "It's something people judge you by. If you have a bad one, you're sad."

For today's teenagers, schoolbags have become a vital symbol of personal taste. Tamsin Millmore, Charlotte Allen and Poppy Roe (my daughter), all 15-year-olds from Lewes, East Sussex, are eager to explain their significance.

"We all wear school uniform," explains Tamsin, "so if you have a different bag, you stand out. Come in with a Safeway carrier and everyone would laugh." Charlotte Allen, 15, is a sporty girl and has a sports-label rucksack. Tamsin shows off a discreet black shoulder bag with cruelly-thin short straps and a small "Kookai" label, which clearly matters: "I'm the only one in my school who has that bag," she says. "Everyone else has one that says Kookai in really big letters."

Poppy has a wide-strap shoulder-bag that took weeks of anguish to select for its specifically businesslike – rather than school-like – simplicity.

The individual look is crucial, but so is the way the girls carry their bags – and it is this aspect that is more worrying.

Levent Caglar, a senior ergonomist with the Furniture Industry Research Association, has made a study of schoolbags and says the best way of carrying them is across both shoulders, rucksack style. The worst way to lug them is on one shoulder alone: "That is bad," Mr Caglar says flatly. "If you maintain that carrying style for long periods with heavier weights; it could damage the vertebral discs or ligaments."

Yet this is exactly what Poppy, Tamsin, Charlotte and all their schoolfriends do, even though they all admit it can be painful. Charlotte has a bad back following a bicycle accident and says she sometimes wears her rucksack "properly" but, more frequently, she slips two straps over one shoulder.

The vast majority of children do the same, according to The National Back Pain Association, because the way you carry your bag – balancing the huge weight of it on one hunched shoulder – is as much of a social indicator as the bag itself.

According to Ian Jameson deputy head of The Bishop Reindorp Church of England School in Guildford, Surrey, 99 per cent of children prefer to carry their bags this way. "It's not cool to use two shoulders," he explains. This may sound ridiculous, but such prejudices are creating a serious problem. By the age of 14, 50 per cent of children suffer back pain.

The National Back Pain Association has now launched a campaign to curb the harm being done to children who carry ill-designed bags badly, thereby straining growing muscles.

Yet Poppy, Tamsin and Charlotte would not be seen dead carrying their bags ergonomically. "Foreign exchange students wear their bags on two shoulders," they chime, "and we don't want to be like that."

Their schoolbags, loaded for a normal day, weigh in at about 8lbs on the kitchen scales. That is relatively light; The Bishop Reindorp School recently sample-tested pupils' bags and found the average weight was 18lbs.

I tell the girls that Mr Caglar thinks that they could have back problems in future from the one-arm style. Will that change their attitude? "Maybe," says Poppy, doubtfully. "Probably not,' says Tamsin.

It is Charlotte who concedes: "People don't realise how much fashion controls a lot of what we wear and what bags we carry. If rucksacks instead of shoulder bags were fashionable, we would probably wear them."

Someone, somewhere, please note.

TASK

Write a detailed article for your school newspaper or parents' magazine in which you describe and explain some of the problems concerning the health, safety and well-being of pupils in secondary schools, and inform parents what can be done to reduce the risks.

Writing to inform, explain and describe 2

Examiner's tip — All three skills might come into play in this task. The examiner will look to see how well you can handle different skills in one piece of writing. When you describe, your purpose is to be clear about the details. Your content might be a presentation of existing hazards in schools. The reader needs to gain a strong and clear impression of how you see the situation. Explanation of the problems will involve some analysis, helping the reader to understand the problems. You will be expected to add some ideas, to go into the problems and think about them, rather than just stating what they are. When you come on to informing, your sense of audience will be important. Be clear what advice you are putting across – don't be woolly or confuse the parents. Your style and tone will need to be courteous and probably formal, and you might take the chance to expand ideas to be even more convincing.

ANSWER

Writing to explain, describe, inform

During some recent studies on schools and the children across the country, scientists have found out how day to day things that the children do and that they wear could be affecting their health.

One of these day to day incidents in school is that of how the children are sitting whilst they work at their desks. Studies have found that the majority of children sit slouching in their chairs as they work. This has dramatic effects on childrens health says Dr John Reid from the department of health. He told us that slouching can cause severe back pain to the children as it bends the bottom of the spine in an awkward unnatural way that tires out the muscles and causes pain in the lower back. This continual "wrong sitting" at desks can also lead to bigger back problems in later life, as the spine becomes accustomed to this position and deforms into this position. Hence this can affect the posture of the child and so cause them to have difficulties in back movement in later times. The only way to stop this problem increasing in number over the years is to inform the children about sitting properly through proper education of this problem to teachers and parents.

Another of these school problems is that of shoes and how they are affecting your children. Shoes are a big thing to kids as if they want to be seen as cool they have to get good fashionable shoes, and this for girls means that they have to get high heels to be in. The reason that they have got to be heels is because they make girls look alot taller and therefore they will look older too. This is all fine of course but these girls are wearing these shoes everyday throughout a school week. This is what the problem is, as when girls wear heels they are in an unnatural position which is arching the bottom of their backs. This is fine for only a day or so to go out in now and then, but as they wear them everyday their backs are becoming deformed in to this arched position. And as they grow older this will affect them more as they will be more likely to get back trouble and this will be quite bad, infact sometimes this back trouble can hamper their movements quite a lot.

Its not just the girls however that get trouble from the shoes they are wearing, as at the moment it is "cool" for boys to not tie their shoes laces as it sort of fits in with the lazy sort of boy image that is currently around. Also the weight of these shoes, which are things like "Kickers" and "Ellesse" which are quite chunky things, add to the trouble that your feet go through just to keep these untied shoes on. This problem has been researched by physiotherapists at hospitals around the U.K. into how your feet cope in keeping untied shoes on. Infact they found out that your feet have to arch to fill as much space in the shoes as possible so that they just don't fall off your feet. This means that your feet are working overtime just so that your shoes stay on them. And so children that do this at school use up more of their youthful energy than is needed to be. However this isn't the only effect of having loose untied shoes, as this arching of the feet can deform them and their structure and cause the children to have feet trouble when they grow older.

Finally another of these health worries at school is that of the surfacing around it. As they are mostly concrete paving slabs in the outside of the school and this quite slippy floor tiling on the inside of the buildings. These can be trouble during the winter months as the rain starts to fall on a regular day to day basis and the surface over which the children have to walk becomes very slippy. This is because the flat, smooth, flooring that we have at school is very hazardous in rain. As there is nothing apart from a thin slippy layer of water for our shoes to grip onto underfoot. This is more of a problem for the younger children as they like to run around and play games like 'chase' during the lunch time hours. This means that these slippy surfaces could pose a risk for them as they sprint across them. And if they slipped, they could infact end up with broken bones from falling. Which can cause long term problems for these children.

So from this explaination of some of the studies that have been made, I have found that some long term effects can happen to the health of children. And so I believe that children should be informed about the trouble of slouching and fashionable shoeware. And finally schools should be designed to cope with these slippy surface troubles.

Examiner's commentary — In this candidate's answer there is a good attempt to write for the audience of parents. He has succeeded with the descriptive element, so that the parents would feel informed of some of the problems. He has selected a few key ideas and gone into them in some detail. The earlier ideas are clearly highly relevant. There is a good effort at explanation, with many aspects of the topic analysed at some length. The weakness in the work is that he has failed to inform parents of what can be done to reduce risks. Remember always to check that you are doing precisely what the rubric requires.

Paragraph structure is good and the style generally appropriate, although the writing is not completely fluent. For most of the exam boards the work would meet the criteria for a grade B.

15

2 Different writing tasks

WRITING TO EXPLORE, IMAGINE AND ENTERTAIN

You are asked to write imaginatively, perhaps in a story or poem or through imagining a scene.
Here you are presented with two poems, one imagining a scene in an urban world, the second a rural scene.

STIMULUS MATERIAL

The Hunchback in the Park Dylan Thomas

The hunchback in the park
A solitary mister
Propped between trees and water
From the opening of the garden lock
That lets the trees and water enter
Until the Sunday sombre bell at dark

Eating bread from a newspaper
Drinking water from the chained cup
That the children filled with gravel
In the fountain basin where I sailed my ship
Slept at night in a dog kennel
But nobody chained him up.

Like the park birds he came early
Like the water he sat down
And Mister they called Hey mister
The truant boys from the town
Running when he had heard them clearly
On out of sound

Past lake and rockery
Laughing when he shook his paper
Hunchbacked in mockery

Through the loud zoo of the willow groves
Dodging the park keeper
With his stick that picked up leaves.

And the old dog sleeper
Alone between nurses and swans
While the boys among willows
Made the tigers jump out of their eyes
To roar on the rockery stones
And the groves were blue with sailors

Made all day until bell time
A woman figure without fault
Straight as a young elm
Straight and tall from his crooked bones
That she might stand in the night
After the locks and the chains

All night in the unmade park
After the railings and shrubberies
The birds the grass the trees the lake
And the wild boys innocent as strawberries
Had followed the hunchback
To his kennel in the dark.

April Rise Laurie Lee

If ever I saw blessing in the air
 I see it now in this still early day
Where lemon-green the vaporous morning drips
 Wet sunlight on the powder of my eye.

Blown bubble-film of blue, the sky wraps round
 Weeds of warm light whose every root and rod
Splutters with soapy green, and all the world
 Sweats with the bead of summer in its bud.

If ever I heard blessing it is there
 Where birds in trees that shoals and shadows are
Splash with their hidden wings and drops of sound
 Break on my ears their crests of throbbing air.

Pure in the haze the emerald sun dilates,
 The lips of sparrows milk the mossy stones,
While white as water by the lake a girl
 Swims her green hand among the gathered swans.

Now, as the almond burns its smoking wick,
 Dropping small flames to light the candled grass;
Now, as my low blood scales its second chance,
 If ever world were blessed, now it is.

TASK

Using your imagination, write about two contrasting scenes, one in an urban setting (towns or cities), the other in a rural setting (the countryside). You may use the poems to give you ideas if you wish, although you do not have to do so. You may write in either prose (continuous writing) or poetry.

Writing to explore, imagine and entertain

Examiner's tip Good and effective imaginative writing requires you to be creative. This means picturing scenes and ideas in your mind – a skill known as visualizing – and then creating a picture of that scene in language. Try to be precise rather than vague, be willing to experiment with language and, above all, attempt to establish a mood and tone in your writing. Marking criteria from the exam boards tend to stress the need to 'shape' writing by using 'stylistic devices'. Examiners will be interested in how well you have been able to choose appropriate and precise vocabulary, whether you have used any images, how well you have used description to bring scenes to life, and so on. Above all try to be original. A common fault with this type of writing is to be predictable, so always try to picture scenes of your own as clearly as you can. Remember also that you are asked to create contrasting scenes in this task.

ANSWER

Urban Life.

She left her apartment, a waft of sugar and fat came by from the doughnut stall. She pushed through the crowds of unimpatient people, and tripped on the uneven, harsh concrete slabs. The fall was brutal on her knees but people continued to struggle round her. She picked her self up and sat on a sturdy metal bench. She considered things around her, like the smell of burnt petrol, from chokeing exhausts, it made every breath feel heavy.

The sky was dismal, clouds of dirty fumes invaded the world above, it was like pollution was slowly covering the sky until finally it would black out everything.

Lonely straggly Beeches stood one by one in neat rows, imprisoned in metal cages, fenced around the thin tree trunks. They were lined up like small children waiting for a bus only it never arrives. Flats were also uniform, all identical with the exception of the odd individual colour. The streets were as straight as a ruler, everything was parralell, each side of the road was like a mirror image of each other.

Rural Area.

He had allready walked for three miles, and as he approched the final field, his foot squelched into the oozing mud. The grass looked brittle and brighter than usual. As the forest of naked trees ended, the wind felt stronger against his face, his nose felt as icy cold and as dead as the landscape looked. Clouds of steam coming from the cattle's warm circulating breaths, they looked like powerful dragons in an icy layer. The bare trees looked eerie and daunting, the branches were blackened with cold, the taller branches stretched up to the clear uninviting sky, and looked higher and higher every time he looked at them.

The frosty air was crisp and fresh, it felt clean and made him feel cold inside when he inhaled. The end of the field and cobble path didn't seem to be getting any closer. But the wind was becoming stronger and slapping him on the face harder every time. The old warn fencing dividing the fields, was starting to show its age, splitting and crumbling as if a wood worm had attacked it. He clambered over the rickety fence and truged over the cobbled path, they crunched and crashed under his feet. The warmth from his home could be seen glowing from the windows of his cottage, and as he opened the rattling door, a heat draught hit him.

Examiner's commentary This candidate has genuinely attempted a contrast based on the movement of two unknown characters. This has provided scope for some powerful description where language is used effectively, if not adventurously. There are some good attempts at imagery, which add considerably to the overall impression and effect. There is clear engagement in the task with some attempt to create and sustain mood, particularly in the rural description. There is, however, some predictable choice of vocabulary, and there are some basic spelling errors which for most of the exam boards might keep the grade at C rather than B level.

2 Different writing tasks

WRITING TO ANALYSE, REVIEW AND COMMENT

The third type of writing which is referred to in the GCSE syllabus is writing to analyse, review and comment. Here you are asked to produce such a piece of writing.

Printed below is a piece of writing from the June 1995 edition of the *Reader's Digest* which talks about an aspect of smoking. It is a fact that smoking is again on the increase among young people.

STIMULUS MATERIAL

How cigarettes cloud your brain

by Lowell Ponte

Let's say you're a smoker, lighting up your first cigarette of the day. Within moments you start to feel the mind-altering changes smoking brings.

Almost everyone, including those who do it, acknowledges the long-term health risks of smoking, especially lung cancer and coronary heart disease. But most smokers perceive the immediate effect of smoking as positive: a stimulant that makes them feel more alert, clear headed and able to focus on work.

But does smoking really have these effects? No: the smoker's perception is mostly an illusion. Take a close look at what smoke does to the brain.

Within ten seconds of your first inhalation, nicotine, a potent alkaloid, passes into your bloodstream, crosses the barrier that protects the brain from most impurities, and begins to act on brain cells. Nicotine molecules fit like keys into the "nicotinic" receptors on the surface of the brain's receptors on the surface of the brain's neurons.

In fact, nicotine fits the same "keyholes" as one of the brain's most important neurotransmitters (signal chemicals), acetylcholine. By mimicking acetylcholine, the 1.5 milligrammes of nicotine obtained from smoking your first cigarette elicit the body's excitation chemicals, including adrenalin (epinephrine) and noradrenalin (norepinephrine). This gives you a rush of stimulation and increases the flow of blood in your brain.

If an electronencephalograph were wired to your head, your EEG would almost immediately record a change in brainwave patterns. Your brain's output of alpha waves – electrical impulses associated with alert relaxation – dips at first but is restored by the time you finish your first cigarette. The sleep-related delta waves and theta waves – involved in emotions, creative imagery and deep thought – grow weaker. But your brain's electrical output surges in beta waves, typically seen during intense concentration and mental agitation.

TEN puffs have flowed through your lungs, and that first cigarette has burned to ash. You feel energised and clear-headed. Are you more sharply focused now than, say, a non-smoking colleague? You may think so, but your improved state of mind is partly due to the fact that you've just ended a period of nicotine deprivation. And you're about to enter another.

Within 30 minutes, the nicotine you've ingested is sharply reduced, and you feel your energy begin to slip away. You light a second cigarette. Again you feel an adrenalin surge, but now the experience is subtly different.

Nicotine triggers a cascade of biochemical changes in the brain. A stress-regulating substance called cortisol is released, along with beta-endorphin, the brain's opiate-like pain reliever. With this second cigarette you begin to feel one of the paradoxes of smoking – that at one dose it can stimulate, at another soothe. You feel muscles throughout your body start to relax, and your pain threshold rises.

THIRTY more minutes pass, and your attention increasingly drifts away from your work and towards that nearby packet of cigarettes. The craving smokers feel for nicotine is more than psychological, more than a habit or a desire of the kind people feel for chocolate. Nicotine prompts brain cells to grow many more nicotinic receptors than they would otherwise. This allows the brain to function normally despite an unnatural amount of acetylcholine-like chemical acting on it. Nicotine thus reshapes the brain so that a smoker feels normal when nicotine floods his or her neurons and abnormal when it doesn't.

Most smokers are engaged in a daily struggle, says Jonathan Foulds, specialist in Tobacco Addiction at St George's Hospital Medical School in London. "They need a constant supply of Nicotine to avoid the poor concentration of withdrawal and in many offices, restaurants, trains and so on, this is unacceptable and must be done covertly. The smokers can't relax."

The American Psychiatric Association classifies smoking withdrawal as a "nicotine-induced organic mental disorder" whose symptoms include anxiety, irritability, anger, restlessness, frustration, insomnia, decreased heart rate and increased appetite.

Several studies have compared active smokers with "deprived" smokers – those suffering nicotine withdrawal – on their ability to perform simple skill tests. These are often cited (and many were funded) by the tobacco industry as evidence that smoking enhances alertness and performance. "What they really show," says Jack Henningfield of the US National Institute on Drug Abuse, "is that nicotine withdrawal causes dramatic mental dysfunction".

IT'S no later than mid-morning when you light your third cigarette. Compared with the first, it tastes flat. If you're like most of the 12.5 million adult Britons who still smoke, you will soon be lighting the next and the next almost by reflex. Smokers average 15 cigarettes a day, meaning nearly 55,000 inhalations a year.

Besides the nicotine, those puffs obtain carbon monoxide. This gas robs the smoker of oxygen by bonding – at least 200 times more tightly than oxygen does – to the haemoglobin that ordinarily delivers oxygen to cells throughout the body. Because of the carbon monoxide, cells cannot prise oxygen atoms loose. If a significant percentage of your haemoglobin were thus made useless by carbon monoxide, you would almost certainly die.

Each cigarette pumps ten to 20 milligrammes of carbon monoxide into your lungs. People typically lose three to nine per cent of their oxygen carrying capacity while smoking. During periods of intense smoking, this loss can reach more than ten per cent, which may slow reaction time and reduce mental awareness.

PSYCHOLOGIST George Spilich and colleagues at Washington College in Maryland decided to find out whether, as many smokers say, smoking helps them to "think and concentrate". Spilich put young non-smokers, active smokers and smokers deprived of cigarettes through a series of tests.

In the first, each subject sat before a computer screen and pressed the space-bar as soon as he or she recognised a target letter among an array of 96. In this simple test, smokers, deprived smokers and non-smokers performed equally well.

The next test was more complex, requiring all to scan sequences of 20 identical letters and respond the instant one of the letters transformed into a different one. Non-smokers were fastest, but under the stimulation of nicotine, active smokers were faster than deprived smokers.

The complexity of the test increased. A third test required people to remember a sequence of letters or numbers and respond when that sequence appeared amid flashed groupings on the screen. In this test of short-term memory, non smokers made the fewest errors, but deprived smokers committed fewer errors than active smokers.

The fourth experiment required people to read a passage, then answer questions about it. Non-smokers remembered 19 per cent more of the most important information than active smokers, and deprived smokers bettered their counterparts who had smoked cigarette just before testing. Active smokers not only tended to have poorer memories but also had trouble differentiating important information from trivial details.

From his final experiment, Spilich got subjects to perform in a computer-generated driving simulator, much like a quick-paced video game. Participants had to operate a steering-wheel, gear lever and accelerator pedal, and cope with unexpected challenges such as twisting roads, the sudden appearance of cars and oil-slicks. By the end of the test, deprived smokers were involved in roughly 67 per cent more rear-end collisions than non-smokers. Smokers who had just had a cigarette did even worse. They were involved in significantly more simulated accidents and three and a half times more rear-end collisions than were non-smokers.

"As our test became more complex," sums up Spilich, "the non-smokers outperformed the smokers by wider and wider margins."

On the basis of this research, Spilich speculates, "a smoker might perform adequately at many jobs – until they got complicated. He could drive a car satisfactorily so long as everything remained routine, but if a tyre blew out at high speed he might not handle the emergency as well as a non-smoker. A smoking airline pilot could fly adequately if no problems arose, but if something went wrong, smoking might impair his mental capacity. If lack of sleep were also a problem, smoking could leave such a pilot relatively impaired – with dangerous consequences."

Consider that the next time you light up the day's first cigarette – and drive your car to work.

Writing to analyse, review and comment

TASK

Use the information from the article and your own views in writing your own article arguing either for or against smoking.

Examiner's tip
It is important to understand the writing skills required here. It's worth just thinking about what they mean. *Review* means making an overall judgement about a topic: in this case, one that you are asked to read about first. It is quite a demanding skill as you are being asked to hold in your mind a number of key ideas all at once. *Analysis* is the skill of examining an issue, of unravelling and interpreting the main points. Then you need to be able to *comment* appropriately on your ideas and findings. This involves making well informed judgements, taking account of the readers so that they can follow your views.

Examiners will want to see evidence of clear planning and organisation, with logical and structured points leading the reader through the main parts of the argument. The writing will need to be relatively formal, with clear progression from one paragraph to another. There will need to be an informed response to the *Reader's Digest* article and use of mature and relevant ideas from the candidate's own experience of smoking as an issue in society.

Note that in the sample answer *it's* is often used incorrectly.

ANSWER

> Smoking.
>
> Many people when introduced to a cigarette are attracted to it's effects. How can this not be? A greater percentage of people today are aware of it's dangers and still persevere. People are no longer guinea pigs and the effects and dangers of smoking are no longer unforeseen. Many, after enjoying this stimulus, have been suffering from it's consequences for years. Smoking is responsible for many deaths, disabilities and illnesses such as Chronic Bronchitis, Emphysema, Cardiovascular disease and lung cancer.
>
> The smoker is playing Russian Roulette with their life. Cigarette smoke consists of more than 4,700 compounds, 43 of which are carcinogens, such as tar. Nicotine a poisonous alkaloid is considered the addicting agent that makes quitting so difficult. 50 mg of an alkaloid on an adults tongue is fatal.
>
> Yet smoking is an escape. Sweet nicotine burning through your veins, muscles relaxing. A smoker can sit back and become more sociable. Because at first your in control, the cigarette is just a friend invited into your bloodstream. Alkaloid; a guest in your brain. Yet after time you are slowly seduced as the craving for Nicotine increases. This is how Nicotine works; slowly and slyly it invades your head. Nicotine molecules in decaying your brain fit perfectly into nicotinic receptors. At first there's a headrush as the increase in adrenalin pumps your blood faster around your body, then there's the feeling of alertness and refreshment. As your body overcomes the nicotine this energy slips away and your fingers fidget for just one more drag. You can't concentrate or be content until Nicotine is pumping around your blood stream.
>
> Your brain has been manipulated. Alkaloid, unknown to the smoker, has altered your brain by increasing the number of Nicotinic receptors. The smoker only feels normal and in control when Nicotine is in their blood.
>
> Nicotine infests your head, it has control it's no longer a guest. Your brain is now it's habitat. You crave it's effects. Sparking up a cigarette becomes as natural as breathing and depriving the brain of this can cause an altered personality; anxiety, irritability, anger, restlessness, frustration, insomnia and a decreased heart rate can take effect. A smoker has a 'Nicotine-induced organic mental disorder'.
>
> An alkaloid can not only enter the body by inhaling but it can be absorbed into the blood stream via your skin. 40,000 non-smokers die every year in America alone through passive smoking. A lack of respect for yourself can prove fatal to others.

2 Different writing tasks

WRITING TO ARGUE, PERSUADE AND INSTRUCT

The fourth type of writing to which your teachers will have referred is writing to argue, persuade and instruct. The task below is an example of such writing in the form of a letter.

STIMULUS MATERIAL

Please will you stop paying to have my people murdered?

There was only one possible name for Friends of the Earth's report on the Amazonian mahogany trade: "Mahogany is Murder".

What follows has been pieced together from the evidence of many different Indians.

Let me tell you how it is with us Indians, and the mahogany cutters.

On March 28th, 1988, about 100 Indians met in a house by a river, to discuss what to do about the timber thieves who were cutting and stealing mahogany trees from their lands.

A boat came up the river. It was the timber cutter, Oscar Branco, with 16 hired gunmen. The men got out and shouted that they had come to kill everyone. They started firing.

The Indians tried to flee in canoes, but many were gunned down. Fourteen Indians, including children, were killed. Twenty-two more were wounded.

Everyone knew who the killers were. Branco was named as the ringleader by Brazil's chief of Federal Police. Eleven of the sixteen gunmen have been identified.

Yet four years have passed and not one has been prosecuted.

Those Indians and their children – their deaths didn't count.

•••

The Indian lands are ours by right forever. No outsider is meant to come into them without our permission. Nobody is supposed to clear the land, or cut trees for timber or break the ground open looking for gold. The law is supposed to protect us and our land.

But they do come, the timber cutters. They come because the mahogany is so precious.

They try all kinds of tricks to get us to part with the timber. Men come in trucks to some Indian villages. They give out radios, torches, T-shirts, biscuits and tins of food. The villagers were very grateful for these gifts.

Some weeks later the men returned. They said that the goods had been given on credit and they had come to collect payment – in trees.

In our Kayapo lands, the timber cutters know the Indians are hostile. So they sneak in and out as quickly as they can. Then they send messengers who say that, as the trees have already been cut down, the Indians can only gain if they take a share of the profits and allow the timber cutters to remove the trees.

•••

Some Indians have been fooled into agreeing to contracts which are not at all to their benefit. Two young Xikrin Indians, who had no authority to speak for their tribe, were persuaded to sign a deal with a big timber company. One of those companies which supplies your British importers.

The deal said that half the wood taken from the forest would be granted free to the company to cover the cost of cutting the trees.

It is the first time anyone's heard of a timber company being paid to cut down trees.

The rest of the trees, worth about £300 each, were to be bought from the Xikrin Indians for just £10 each.

But when the final settlement came the Indians got no money, only a bill claiming that they owed the timber company £6,000 for 'merchandise'.

•••

It is when we Indians resist the invasion of our lands that the killing starts.

During an argument, a timber cutter threw an Indian woman's baby into a river where it drowned.

A film crew met eleven timber cutters armed with shotguns and entering the forest at the start of an Indian hunt.

Even if the timber cutters do not murder us with guns, they have other ways to kill our people.

The mahogany trees grow far apart so the timber cutters hack roads through the forest to reach them. Nearly half of our people have died from diseases brought by the timber cutters since first contact with the outside world.

While our people die, the forest disappears forever.

Many other trees are damaged in the death struggles of the big mahoganies.

We should not cut the trees. The trees give the fruit we eat. We want the honey from the trees, the fruits and all there is to be eaten in the forest. Without the trees there is no game for us to hunt.

It is greed that is killing us, and the trees and the animals.

Your greed for mahogany.

You in Britain buy more than half the mahogany Brazil produces.

Look! That deep red glow in your new mahogany dinner table is the blood of murdered Indians.

Listen! The clatter of your mahogany lavatory seat is the gunfire that killed Indian children.

You must do all you can to help those who are fighting this evil trade.

We don't believe that after reading this you could ever contemplate buying mahogany again. But if we are to halt the illegal trade you must help us force importers and retailers to change their attitudes.

We have to awaken MPs and Government to the scandal. Friends of the Earth campaigns locally, nationally, internationally and tirelessly against the cynical timber trade which is accelerating the demise of the Earth's last rainforests and their peoples. We've already helped persuade the World Bank to stop funding logging projects in primary rainforest areas. Since our campaign began, British imports of tropical timber have dropped by a third. But we need to do so much more. Time is running out. People are dying. The forest is vanishing. Please join us. Please do it now.

Writing to argue, persuade and instruct 2

TASK

The advertisement by Friends of the Earth says, "We have to awaken MPs and Government to the scandal".

Write a letter to your MP at The House of Commons, London, SW1A 2DG, expressing your opposition to the mahogany trade. You may use the information in the advertisement to support your arguments, but you should also use your own ideas.

Remember that this is a formal letter and you should set it out appropriately.

WJEC 1996

Examiner's tip

When you are asked to write a formal letter, it is very important to set it out using the proper conventions of such a letter. It is also essential to understand exactly what kind of writing task you are being asked to complete. Here, because you have to express opposition to the mahogany trade, you are writing to argue, and to persuade your reader.

The examiner will be looking to see how well you have taken your reader into account. You are expected to write in a way that is controlled and well organised. For the higher marks you will need to use a range of sentence structures and your paragraphing, spelling and punctuation should be accurate.

ANSWER

Miss Sophie Beavers
28 Devizes Road
Swindon
Wiltshire.

Monday 3rd November 1997.

Ms Julia Drown
Labour MP for Swindon
The House of Commons
London
SW1A 2DG.

Dear Ms Drown,

I am a student who usually shows very little interest in environmental issues, but I have been struck and am rather concerned about the effects of the mahogany trade in Brazil, and suggesting that it is causing Amazonian Indians due to British greed.

I became aware of the enormity of the situation when I read an advertisement produced by Friends of the Earth. This divulged the distress, hardship and loss that the Indians faced in their own domain due to the gluttony of the timber cutters.

On 28th March, 1983, one hundred Indians attended a discussion about the timber thieves stealing mahogany trees from their land. A boat containing a timber thief and sixteen gunmen came up the river and shot and killed fourteen Indians (including children), and injured twenty two others for no apparent reason. The Brazilian Federal Police knew who the gunmen were, yet after four years none of them have been prosecuted. What is their justification to commit cold-blooded murder?

The Indians stand in the way of the timber cutters' wealth, yet it is they who hold the key to the Indians' destruction. The Indians rely on the mahogany tree for their survival. They bear honey and fruits that the Indians eat and the game that they hunt. The trees are the Indians' home. When the trees die so do the Indians. A quote from the article which compelled me to express my feelings about the issue to you was: "Look! That deep red glow in your new mahogany dinner table is the blood of murdered Indians. Listen! The clatter of your mahogany knitting knit is the gunfire that killed Indian children." These are vivid images of pain and death which are linked to everyday household items, which I believe emphasizes their importance.

I hope that through this letter you are now aware of the scandal that is occurring and that you will use the power that the constituency of Swindon have presented you, to take action against the Brazilian Mahogany Trade. Britain buys more than half the mahogany that Brazil produces. Although tropical timber imports have been cut by a third this is not enough as many Indians are still dying through this cynical trade.

Please take action against British greed in order to save not only suppressed animals, but human lives too; as one Indian said, "Please will you stop paying to have my people murdered?"

Yours Sincerely,

Sophie Beavers
SOPHIE BEAVERS (MISS)

Examiner's commentary

This candidate's letter is written in a controlled and concise style with an excellent structure. The sentence structure, the spelling and the punctuation are all very assured, the tone is polite but firm and as a result it would have the desired effect of being persuasive.

Above all, there is an excellent paragraph structure: each paragraph is linked, showing a logical pattern of thought.

She has used the material effectively without becoming over-dependent on it. The only criticism that an examiner might have is that there could have been a stronger statement of the argument against the mahogany trade in the second paragraph, but overall it is a clear and persuasive piece of writing, worthy of marks for an A grade.

2 Different writing tasks

A PARTICULAR SKILL – WRITING A SUMMARY

STIMULUS MATERIAL

A particular skill which is frequently tested is the important skill of summary writing. Below is an example: read the passage carefully and then complete the task which follows it.

'Men can't stand successful women'

They may say they're thrilled by our achievements, but the truth, argues feminist **Maeve Haran**, is that they're often threatened by women.

I know a couple, both famous actors, whose faces are often splashed all over the TV – but rarely at the same time. One moment she may have a starring role, while he is temporarily in the shadows. Then it's his turn for the big time, and she'll be back waiting by the phone. But what's fascinating is the different ways they react to the seesaw of television fame. When he's up and she's down she seems genuinely glad for him and boasts to everyone how well he's doing. When the roles are reversed he sulks and moves the conversation on.

And yet, if you challenge him with this, he's horrified. 'But I love my wife's success,' he enthuses. 'I'm really proud of her.' Oh yes? This, you see, is a tricky cat to coax out of the bag. It's unfashionable in these caring, sharing times for men to admit to feeling threatened. So you can't pay too much attention to what they say. Watch what they do instead.

How often does a woman prepare the ground for her man to feel good about himself? By creating little openings for him to shine conversationally, encouraging him to recount stories she's heard so often she could tell them better than him, and – if he's too modest to do it himself (ha!) – by making sure the assembled gathering knows of his most recent success. And does he return the favour? Does he demand to know if everyone's heard of Doreen's latest triumph at the office? Does he hell.

Men, you see, have ways of dealing with uppity spouses. They interrupt them. They change the subject. And later, in the privacy of the matrimonial bedroom, they accuse them of showing off, of hijacking the evening and boring the pants off everyone. The wife in question, having just sat through 45 minutes on the current state of the ball-bearing industry, is gobsmacked.

And woe betide the woman who takes him along to some event where she's in her element and he's just The Husband. Does he make the effort to strike up conversations because he can see she's having a good time? No, he sulks and stands apart, staring into his glass or reading the host's old copies of *Reader's Digest* until he finally announces at 10pm that he's going, but she can stay on without him if she wants. Grrr!

And these are far from being isolated incidents. Robin Skynner, the family therapist who co-writes with John Cleese, says the most common problem among couples he's seen is husbands who are passively resisting, and emotionally withdrawing from, wives who've become confident and independent.

But the worst thing of all for men seems to be when an apparently happy homemaker suddenly becomes an independent woman. When the wife of a well-known writer developed a successful career in her late thirties he confided to me that it had shaken him to the core, challenging his deeply held perception of himself as the breadwinner, the person around whom everything revolved. He had to stop seeing her as Little Wifey and realise that, instead of devoting herself to his wants and needs, she now had demands of her own.

So why is it so hard for men to genuinely glory in the achievements of the women in their lives? Are they terrified that our success will reduce them to chief handbag carrier?

I suppose it comes down to identity. The old Mighty Warrior syndrome. So much of male self-esteem seems to be tied up in the public acknowledgement of them as winners. And if the woman they're married to is recognised by society as equally, or even more, successful, they see themselves as automatically relegated to the second division.

Mind you, on a practical level, maybe men are right to be worried. Since time immemorial, women have made sacrifices so men are able to spring into the big wide world unencumbered by domestic worries. Now we're asking them to return the favour. To share the housework and the childcare when they'd rather be watching the rugby. To come home and read *Postman Pat's Busy Day* when they'd rather be 'networking' with the lads in the Frog and Ferret, and to man the microwave while we go away on business trips. And that hurts. We're even asking them to confront their own notions of success – which often means staying at work till 9pm because that's part of the ethos – and admitting they have obligations to us as well. And that hurts too.

The bad news is, chaps, that things are only going to get worse. Women are going to ask for more in the future. So far we've tended to let men off the hook. We've been far too understanding We've tried to protect you from the harsh realities of a truly equal marriage. But as women become more successful and independent, the balance of power in relationships is shifting. It's no surprise that approximately 70 per cent of divorce petitions are brought by women – probably fed up with nagging men to cook the evening meal.

Women have learned something new in the last 20 years – that there are joys and satisfactions outside the home as well as inside it. So why can't men learn something too? That if they buried more of their identity in home and family and less of it in winning at work, they might end up happier and saner individuals. Then, instead of begrudging us our achievements, they would be able to enjoy basking in reflected glory. Just as we do in theirs.

A particular skill – writing a summary

TASK

Now you have read 'Men can't stand successful women', write about 200–250 words in which you summarise Maeve Haran's criticisms of men and her explanations for their behaviour.

Use your own words as far as possible.

MEG 1996

Examiner's tip This task involves close reading skills. When you are asked to summarise a passage, it is important before you do anything else to check exactly what you are being asked to summarise. Summaries always ask you to retrieve information from what you have read. The skill is to show that you can find the points – many weaker candidates will fall into the trap of trying to cover everything.

There are two other skills involved: expressing the points in your own words wherever possible and, for the higher levels, making inferences. This means that you can interpret a point, showing what it suggests as opposed to setting it down literally

ANSWER

> **'Men can't stand Successful women'**
>
> Maeve Haran's article criticises men for being jealous of their wives and for not publically congratulating them when they achieve something. Men put on a front - 'I'm really proud of her', but during a conversation with other people will change the subject or interrupt their wives to stop them from getting all the attention. In private, later, the husband tends to chastise their wives for 'boring the pants off of everyone' or 'hijacking the evening', even if the main focus of the evening has been on a subject that the husband is interested in. This takes away some of the wifes self confidence, and may deter her from speaking out again.
>
> At parties held by associates of the female, the male tends to sulk and purposely try not to enjoy himself. He also wants to go home early, and may even give an ultimatum, 'you can stay, but I'm going'. The male may feel threatened if he is not the prominent partner for an evening.
>
> Another factor that annoys the husband is when the wife wants to gain a little independence and go out to work. This challenges the males breadwinning role and means that she won't be at home to cater for his every domestic need.
>
> Men don't want their wives to be as successful or even more so, than them as they feel it means that they are demoted 'to the second division' or becoming 'chief handbag carrier'.
>
> Domestic roles have been changed. If women are going to go out to work then they will have less time and energy for domestic chores. This means that men will have to help out, and donning an apron won't do much for them in the masculinity stakes. It also means that men will have to be more interested in home life, instead of working late and trying to prove themselves at work.
>
> Men are just going to have to accept their wives achievements and be glad for them. They should share in the glory and co-operate with their wives requests, if men don't want the 70 per cent of divorce petitions put in by women to rise.

Examiner's commentary Summaries are usually marked according to the number of relevant points that a candidate has made. The mark schemes are always generous. They often list a large number of points that could be made, but state that candidates are expected to identify only a certain number of them.

This answer is quite good at summarising the criticisms of men made by the writer. The first four paragraphs all contain relevant points. However, the explanations are not so clear. Re-read the final two paragraphs. Can you see that these seem to be answering a different question, explaining what will happen now, rather than giving the explanations for the behaviour of men? So, remember, it is very important to check that what you are writing is precisely what is required in the question.

3 Responding to different kinds of stimulus material

This section is all about "responding to stimuli" – or, put more simply, doing the tasks set. It is introduced by a basic comprehension test and then different types of stimuli are used, including literary, media and non-fiction. You will find detailed examination tasks (or questions) with some examples of responses (or answers) written by real pupils.

If you really want a challenge, why not have a go at the tasks yourself before you look at the responses of the pupils?

At the end of the section see if you have been able to identify the main principles involved in responding to English exam questions. In English you are never marked for getting answers right or wrong. Using and understanding English – your own language – can never be as simple as that. So try to use this section to grasp what sorts of things you will be marked for.

COMPREHENSION

Comprehension is a general word which means "understanding". In exams you are asked to read passages, and to show that you understand them you are then asked a series of questions about the meanings and language.

It is important that you understand some of the skills involved in answering comprehension questions; what is most important is that you learn how to interpret the types of questions that you are asked.

First, let's look at a comprehension passage and the answers that have been written by one pupil. Read the following passage carefully and then answer the questions that follow. You should try to answer all the questions and, as far as possible, to answer in your own words.

The travel writer, Michael Palin, is recounting a journey from the North to South Poles. Near the start of his journey, he and his group of travellers are on Day 6, and have reached Kap Wik which is still in the far north. The passage describes his reception at the home of Harald Solheim, who lives near the Arctic Circle.

STIMULUS MATERIAL

DAY 6 KAP WIK TO LONGYEARBYEN

It's 2.45 in the morning when we arrive at Harald Solheim's hut. A tall wooden frame hung with seal carcasses stands on a slight rise, more prominent than the cabin itself, which is set lower down, out of the wind. The first surprise is Harald himself. Instead of some grizzly bearded old-timer, a tall, pale, studious figure comes out to welcome us. He does have a beard, but attached as it is to long, aquiline features the effect is more rabbi than trapper. The second surprise is how benignly and agreeably he copes with the appearance of ten tired and hungry travellers in the middle of the night. First we fill up his miniscule hallway with our boots and bags, then we burst his sitting-room to the seams, whilst he heats up some stew on a wood-burning stove. His wood supply, neatly stacked in a workshop, is driftwood, probably from the Russian coast. His electricity supply is wind-generated.

He fetches out a leg of smoked reindeer which is quite delicious and over this and a mixture of stew, smoked salmon, Aquavit (the local spirit) and Glenmorangie whisky we thaw out and swap stories. Harald offers advice, comment and information, liberally laced with dry humour. It's like some wonderfully chaotic tutorial.

Around about 4.30 a.m. some of us start looking a little anxiously for the dormitory. Harald explains the arrangements. In a next-door room he has four bunk-beds and floor space for two. There is more space on the floor of his workshop. Everyone else will have to sleep in the sitting-room with him. There is one sit-down loo, but as this is a bag that has to be emptied men are requested to use the Great Outdoors whenever possible, but to refrain from peeing on the side

24

Comprehension 3

of the house from which he draws his water supply. For cleaning teeth and washing he recommends the snow.

When I wake, it's half-past eleven. The sitting-room resembles some Viking Valhalla with recumbent Norwegians scattered about and Harald sprawled on the sofa like a warrior slain in battle. Then the telephone rings. Last night my tired brain was so busy romanticizing Harald's existence that I hadn't noticed the phone, or the remote control for the matt-black hi-fi, or the visitor's book, or the collection of Rachmaninov piano concertos on CD, signed 'To Harald from Vladimir Askenazy'. Is it all a dream? Have we been hi-jacked in the night to some apartment in Oslo? I stumble outside clutching my toothbrush and there is the reassuring reality of empty mountains and frozen seas stretching as far as the eye can see.

I scrub snow all over my face and neck. A refreshing shock which dispels any lurking hangover. When I get back indoors Harald is off the phone and preparing coffee. This autumn, he tells me, he will be celebrating 15 years at Kap Wik. He has family in Norway, but they don't visit much. His closest neighbours are the Russians at the mining town of Pyramiden, 18 miles away. He reads a lot, 'Almost everything except religious literature' and hunts seal, reindeer, Arctic fox (a pelt will fetch around £80) and snowgeese, ' "Goose Kap Wik" was served to the King and Queen of Norway,' he informs me, with quiet satisfaction.

'So it's a busy life in the middle of nowhere?'

Harald shrugs. 'Some years I don't see a living soul from autumn to July.'

I ask him if he has ever felt the need for companionship. A woman around the house perhaps.

'It's... er...,' he smiles at his sudden inarticulacy... 'it's not easy to explain in Norwegian... but any woman mad enough to come here...'

He never finishes the sentence. The sound of a distant helicopter brings him to his feet.

'It's my mail', he explains, almost apologetically, as a Sea King helicopter clatters into sight across the fiord.

After a late lunch and more stories our caravan is repacked and relaunched. Harald, smiling, waves us away. I don't really understand why a man of such curiosity, fluency and culture should want to chase animals around Spitsbergen, but I feel he rather enjoys being an enigma, and though he is no hermit he is one of a rare breed of truly independent men.

The rest of the journey is less eventful. The slopes are not as fierce, and the snow is turning to slush in some of the valleys. It's becoming almost routine to turn off one glacier onto another, to roar up snowbound mountain passes and see the seals plop back into their ice-holes as we cross the fiords.

We stop for a while at the spot where Patti had an adventure on the way up to Ny Alesund. She lost her way in a 'white-out' and was not found for almost an hour. I hope this isn't an omen for the long journey ahead.

Although we make fast progress towards Longyearbyen, the weather has not finished with us. Turning into the broad valley that leads to the town we are hit full in the face by a blizzard of stinging wet snow and as Heinrich accelerates for home it makes for a hard and uncomfortable end to the ride.

After five and a half hours travelling we see through the murk the first lights of Longyearbyen, and the snowmobiles screech clumsily along the wet highway.

It's half-past ten and we have reached our first town, 812 miles from the North Pole.

3 Responding to different kinds of stimulus material

QUESTIONS

1. In the writing, there is a lot of evidence of the type of life that Harald lived. Describe his way of life, giving examples of the evidence available in the passage.

2. The writer uses a variety of detail to give an impression of Harald's character. Show how his character is created through:
   - physical description;
   - the account of Harald's relations with the group of travellers;
   - the account of his possessions;
   - his attitude to life.

3. How successfully has the writer used language to describe the scene and to create the mood and atmosphere of the place?

4. In your own words explain the meanings of the words and phrases printed below in bold type:

   "The second surprise is **how benignly and agreeably** he copes with the appearance of ten tired and hungry travellers in the middle of the night."

   "Harald offers advice, comment and information, **liberally laced with dry humour**."

   "… but I feel he rather enjoys **being an enigma**."

5. This extract describes one small part of the writer's journey. What are the features in the writing that would make you interested in following the story of the rest of the journey?

ANSWERS

Here are a pupil's answers to the comprehension questions. As you read them, try to ask yourself these questions about the skills used:
- Has he shown understanding of the passage?
- Has he been able to select relevant parts of the passage to answer the questions precisely?
- Has he supported his answers with adequate evidence, through close reference to examples in the writing?
- Does his own written expression help to get across his meanings?

To save you from looking back at the questions on each occasion, these are repeated for you at the start of each answer:

1. In the writing, there is a lot of evidence of the type of life that Harald lived. Describe his way of life, giving examples of the evidence available in the passage.

> 1. Harold lives in an isolated place. He lives an almost solitary existence, only seeing a few people a year. ("Some years I don't see anyone from Autumn to July.") He lives off the food he can hunt from around the mountains and valleys where he lives. As he is further north than the most northern towns he suffers greatly from the cold. He hunts the animals that live in this area; seals, reindeer, salmon, and does quite well from them. As well as living quite a remote and basic life, which is shown because he has no proper toilet and collects his water from the roof of his house, he also has quite a modern furnished home with plenty of comforts,

26

Comprehension 3

> having things like a remote controlled hi-fi, telephone and large numbers of CD's. He has quite good links to other people. He has his post delivered by a helicopter and he has his phone, but if he had an accident outside the house he probably wouldn't be able to receive any outside assistance.
>
> He has taken advantage of the area he lives in to help equip his home and to help him live. This is shown in the way his wood supply is probably driftwood from the Russian coast and his electricity supply is wind-generated.
>
> Even though Harold's life is one of loneliness, he welcomes visitors with great hospitality. This is shown by the way that he offers good food, Aquavit, and whisky. His way of life is also quite cultured, as he listens to Rachmaninov piano concertos on CD. As well as listening to music, he also seems to have a life where he is a constant reader, perhaps this is to stimulate his mind as he is on his own for the majority of the time.

Examiner's commentary

In this answer the pupil has used a variety of points to show different features of his way of life. Clearly he has gone through the passage and identified the main points. These take account of Harald's surroundings and the way he treats his visitors. Thus, there is good use of the evidence.

2 The writer uses a variety of detail to give an impression of Harald's character. Show how his character is created through:
   - physical description;
   - the account of Harald's relations with the group of travellers;
   - the account of his possessions;
   - his attitude to life.

> 2. When the party reaches Harold's hut it is obvious the author is expecting a very rugged, burly man with a beard, tangled hair and weathered skin. Harold, however, is not the man of the image in the author's mind. He turns out to be "a tall, pale, studious figure." This, plus his rabbi beard, seems to show him to be educated and quite sophisticated.

27

3 Responding to different kinds of stimulus material

ANSWERS

His reactions to the appearance of the travellers, in the middle of the night, is genial, with an even temper. They were expecting a stereotype of the local people, rugged and grizzly, but instead he is kind and friendly ("how benignly and agreably he copes with the appearence of ten tired and hungry travellers"). Also, the way he relates to his guests, by listening to and entertaining them, proves him to be an excellent host. Once the party has sat down, to a meal that Harold has prepared, Harold is described as giving "advice, comment and information, liberally laced with dry humour." This might mean that he has a good relationship with the travellers, he can set up an instant friendship, by making himself very popular. But in the way he treats these strangers in his home, it is like he has known them all his life, so he is trusting, and doesn't expect them to do any wrong.

His possessions show him to be a well-educated and modern man with a lot of time to kill. I think although Harold does like and enjoy the outdoors, he also likes the comfort of his own home and he likes some luxuries, but when you think that he possesses up to date facilities like the CDs and the phone, as well as the books, then these may suggest that he is lonely because he cannot relate to or communicate to other people a lot.

His attitude to life coupled with his chosen place of residence makes him seem something of a loner, but completely independent and in control of his own life.

Examiner's commentary

Again, the strength of this answer is that the pupil has been methodical. He has treated each section of the question separately and interpreted features of Harald's character from the evidence available.

3 How successfully has the writer used language to describe the scene and to create the mood and atmosphere of the place?

> 3. I think the writer has been quite successful in his use of description. Much of the description is quite concise, but the adjectives used are in order to help us create a clear picture in our minds, eg "grizzly bearded."

Comprehension 3

ANSWERS

> The scene at first seems very primitive, which is shown through description of 'A tall wooden frame hung with seal carcasses,' and the use of the word 'hut' seems in keeping with the archaic scene. This illusion is shattered by the eloquence and humour of the educated dweller's speech.
>
> The atmosphere is one of desolation, portrayed by the picture of "empty mountains" and the way that the helicopter "clatters" into sight. Also, the time of day helps me to create the mood, and then the primitive feeling returns in the description of the toilet and washing facilities, which involve snow, a small bag and a toothbrush. This theme is carried through in a description of the sitting rooms as a "Viking Valhalla" and in the image of Harold as a "warrior slain in battle." This primitive, Northern Viking impression is changed by the presence of the modern conveniences, but the desolation returns when Harold says that some years he sees no-one for six months and that his nearest neighbour lives eighteen miles away. Altogether, the lonely mood is helped by the friendly atmosphere created when Harold has company. One other thing you notice is that it is all written in the present tense, which makes the action feel as if it is happening.

Examiner's commentary

This is a successful answer particularly in the way that the pupil has shown how the atmosphere is created. There are sufficient references to the techniques of language used.

4 In your own words explain the meanings of the words and phrases printed below in bold type:

"The second surprise is how **benignly and agreeably** he copes with the appearance of ten tired and hungry travellers in the middle of the night."

> This means that he welcomed the travellers warmly, in a friendly way. He was calm and settling, reassuring towards the ten of them.

"Harald offers advice, comment and information, **liberally laced with dry humour**."

> This means that his advice, comments and information always have a bit of wit in them, like a joke to keep the listener interested in what was said.

29

3 Responding to different kinds of stimulus material

ANSWERS

"... but I feel he rather enjoys **being an enigma**."

> He liked to be a man of contradictions. He kept things secret, and so he was not easy to understand.

Examiner's commentary

The pupil has understood the vocabulary and been able to explain the meanings concisely.

5 This extract describes one small part of the writer's journey. What are the features in the writing that would make you interested in following the story of the rest of the journey?

> 5. I found this passage very interesting and I personally would enjoy reading on. I become interested in the adventures, problems and discoveries that the travellers will make on their journey. I get the impression that if I do read on, the interest will be kept up by the detailed description about his surroundings, and especially about the characters who he comes across. At the end of this extract, I feel that I have got to know Harold, and I predict that there will be many more people who will be described just as well so that I will get to know them just as if I was on the journey too.
>
> Harold's life seems one of repetitiveness: no opportunities crop up each day, few distractions of other humans, very cut off from the outside world. His life will carry on all the time, the door always open as a welcoming sight for all weary travellers passing through his route. I get the feeling that there will be lots more people in other parts of the world and so we will get variety of people in the book. This is what makes me want to read on.

Examiner's commentary

These questions are always difficult because they are so open-ended. This pupil has answered the question well. His reasons for wanting to read on are relevant to the strengths of the passage. He makes points about the qualities of the passage, particularly the way that it deals with understanding of an unusual lifestyle. This is preferable to statements which simply say "I like the passage", or "I would like to read on because it was interesting."

Literary stimulus 3

At some point in your GCSE course you will study pre-twentieth century literature; it may be for one of the examination papers or it might be for a piece of coursework.

Printed below is an extract from *Jane Eyre*, a novel which was written in the nineteenth century by Charlotte Brontë.

Read the extract carefully and then consider the question that follows it.

PRE-TWENTIETH CENTURY LITERARY STIMULUS

STIMULUS MATERIAL

JANE EYRE
by Charlotte Brontë

DURING THESE EIGHT years my life was uniform: but not unhappy, because it was not inactive. I had the means of an excellent education placed within my reach; a fondness for some of my studies, and a desire to excel in all, together with a great delight in pleasing my teachers, especially such as I loved, urged me on: I availed myself fully of the advantages offered me. In time I rose to be the first girl of the first class; then I was invested with the office of a teacher; which I discharged with zeal for two years: but at the end of that time, I altered.

Miss Temple, through all the changes, had thus far continued superintendent of the seminary: to her instruction I owed the best part of my acquirements; her friendship and society had been my continual solace; she stood me in the stead of mother, governess, and, latterly, companion. At this period she married, removed with her husband (a clergyman, and excellent man, almost worthy of such a wife) to a distant county, and consequently was lost to me.

From the day she left I was no longer the same: with her was gone every settled feeling, every association that had made Lowood in some degree a home to me. I had imbibed from her something of her nature and much of her habits: more harmonious thoughts: what seemed better regulated feelings had become the inmates of my mind. I had given in allegiance to duty and order; I was quiet; I believed I was content: to the eyes of others, usually even to my own, I appeared a disciplined and subdued character.

But destiny, in the shape of the Rev Mr Nasmyth, came between me and Miss Temple: I saw her in her travelling dress step in to a post chaise, shortly after the marriage ceremony; I watched the chaise mount the hill and disappear beyond its brow; and then retired to my own room, and there spent in solitude the greatest part of the half-holiday granted in honour of the occasion.

I walked about the chamber most of the time. I imagined myself only to be regretting my loss, and thinking how to repair it; but when my reflections were concluded, and I looked up and found that the afternoon was gone, and evening far advanced, another discovery dawned on me, namely, that in the interval I had undergone a transforming process; that my mind had put off all it had borrowed of Miss Temple – or rather that she had taken with her the serene atmosphere I had been breathing in her vicinity – and that now I was left in my natural element, and beginning to feel the stirring of old emotions. It did not seem as if a prop were withdrawn, but rather as if a motive were gone: it was not the power to be tranquil which had failed me, but the reason for tranquillity was no more. My world had for some years been in Lowood: my experience had been of its rules and systems; now I remembered that the real world was wide, and that a varied field of hopes and fears, of sensations and excitements, awaited those who had courage to go forth into its expanse, to seek real knowledge of life amidst its perils.

I went to my window, opened it and looked out. There were two wings of the building; there was the garden; there were the skirts of Lowood; there was the hilly horizon. My eye passed all other objects to rest on those most remote, the blue peaks: it was those I longed to surmount; all within their boundary of rock and heat seemed prison-ground, exile limits. I traced the white road winding round the base of one mountain, and vanishing in a gorge between the two: how I longed to follow it further! I recalled the time when I had travelled that very road in a coach; I remembered descending that hill at twilight: an age seemed to have elapsed since the day which brought me first to Lowood, and I had never

3 Responding to different kinds of stimulus material

quitted it since. My vacations had all been spent at school: Mrs Reed had never sent for me to Gateshead; neither she nor any of her family had ever been to visit me. I had no communication by letter or message with the outer world; school rules, school duties, school habits and notions, and voices and faces, and phrases, and costumes, and preferences, and antipathies: such was what I knew of existence. And now I felt that it was not enough: I tired of the routine of eight years in one afternoon. I desired liberty; for liberty I gasped; for liberty I uttered a prayer; it seemed scattered on the wind then faintly blowing. I abandoned it and framed a humbler supplication; for change, stimulus; that petition, too, seemed swept off into vague space: "Then," I cried, half desperate, "grant me at least a new servitude!"

TASK

In this extract Jane is reflecting on her earlier life. What feelings does she convey to you about that early life? You should refer in detail to and use quotations from the extract to illustrate the points you wish to make.

ANSWER

Extract of Jane Eyre.

The first impression I receive from reading through the text, is that the early stage of Jane Eyre's life is devoted to the realisation of her own self.

The passage opens by conveying feelings of contentment of security and warmth. These feelings are transmitted to me by the use of strong nouns, 'desire' and 'delight'. As well as the happiness, I feel there is an underlying feeling of restricted urges. 'During these eight years of my life was uniform,' this is recognised by Jane but as it is infitting with the way she leads her life this fact remains unchanged.

She is in awe of Miss Temple, she feels that it is this remarkable woman that is responsible for all her admirable character traits ' I had imbibed from her something of her nature and much of her habits'. Jane feels happy to have gained these as it is a positive transformation and growth. She believed that she owned the traits and not have had them installed.

The beginning of her discovery starts when her teacher is removed, this instigates the feeling of displacement, her only security and familiarity dispersed'. Great sadness and depression follows and this is spurred whilst watching teacher leave as she feels a part of her is leaving too, 'there spent in solitude the greatest part of the half-holiday granted in honor of the occasion'. This period of time is used for reflection, at this point she acknowledges the effect that Miss

Literary stimulus 3

> Temple had. Her original self begins to return and becomes comfortable – even preferable as the discovery of "wide variety of experiences on offer in a new unsheltered world. 'a varied field of hopes and fears'. Within her feelings of excitement and anticipation again began to stir.
> A future filled with knowledge, desperate for adventure, a cry for freedom.

Examiner's commentary There are two particular threads to the question that need to be noted. The main thrust of the question requires you to write about Jane's early life and her feelings about it. You should also pay attention to the requirement for quotation and detailed reference.

The answer that is printed above does this quite well. It uses quotation and takes us systematically through the extract analysing as it goes. There is a clear statement in the opening paragraph, "the realisation of her own self". It is Jane's realisation of her own self, most especially on the afternoon of the departure of Miss Temple which is then examined.

There are weaknesses of language and these would have to be taken into account when marking this writing. Attempts to use a wide range of vocabulary occasionally result in rather odd misuse of words. In terms of structure the writing also comes to a rather abrupt end and certainly lacks a full conclusion.

As we have already mentioned, often in English exams you are given a passage of literature or a poem to read and then asked to write in an imaginative way using what you have read as a starting point.

In this case you are going to be given a question which simply asks you to develop a piece of your own writing based on an idea or a theme in the original passage.

You are asked to read an extract from the novel *A Portrait of the Artist as a Young Man* by James Joyce. This is a well known passage about a young boy receiving a beating at the hands of a cruel teacher. The setting is a religious school in Ireland. The task set at the end of the passage asks you, in a rather general way, to write about an incident involving a teacher and a pupil.

First read the passage, then look at the writing task and consider the options open to you. An example of writing is given.

TWENTIETH CENTURY LITERARY STIMULUS

To set the scene – the Prefect of Studies, Father Dolan, has visited the classroom of Father Arnall. A severe disciplinarian, he has already beaten one boy in the class for doing badly in his Latin grammar. In this passage he turns his attention to Stephen Dedalus, the central character in the story.

STIMULUS MATERIAL

– You, boy, who are you?
Stephen's heart jumped suddenly.
– Dedalus, sir.
– Why are you not writing like the others?
– I... my...
He could not speak with fright.
– Why is he not writing, Father Arnall?
– He broke his glasses, said Father Arnall, and I exempted him from work.

3 Responding to different kinds of stimulus material

> – Broke? What is this I hear? What is this your name is? said the prefect of studies.
> – Dedalus, sir.
> – Out here, Dedalus. Lazy little schemer. I see schemer in your face. Where did you break your glasses?
> Stephen stumbled into the middle of the class, blinded by fear and haste.
> – Where did you break your glasses? repeated the prefect of studies.
> – The cinderpath, sir.
> – Hoho! The cinderpath! cried the prefect of studies. I know that trick.
> Stephen lifted his eyes in wonder and saw for a moment Father Dolan's whitegrey not young face, his baldy whitegrey head with fluff at the sides of it, the steel rims of his spectacles and his nocoloured eyes looking through the glasses. Why did he say he knew that trick?
> – Lazy idle little loafer! cried the prefect of studies. Broke my glasses! An old schoolboy trick. Out with your hand this moment!
> Stephen closed his eyes and held out in the air his trembling hand with the palm upwards. He felt the prefect of studies touch it for a moment at the fingers to straighten it and then the swish of the sleeve of the soutane as the pandybat was lifted to strike. A hot burning stinging tingling blow like the loud crack of a broken stick made his trembling hand crumple together like a leaf in the fire; and at the sound and the pain scalding tears were driven into his eyes. His whole body was shaking with fright, his arm was shaking and his crumpled burning livid hand shook like a loose leaf in the air. A cry sprang to his lips, a prayer to be let off. But though the tears scalded his eyes and his limbs quivered with pain and fright he held back the hot tears and the cry that scalded his throat.
> – Other hand! shouted the prefect of studies.

(N.B. James Joyce was a writer who experimented with his writing by not using speech marks for direct speech. You are advised to use speech marks in your writing. You can remind yourself of the use of speech marks by consulting p8.)

TASK

Write about an incident involving a teacher and a pupil.

> **Examiner's tip**
> Notice, as in this case here, that you are often not given very precise instructions for an imaginative writing task. One of the skills you must use is to interpret the question and see if you can think of an original idea. You are sometimes given some extra guidance which, in this case might be as follows:
> "You could write about an imagined event as part of a story or, if you prefer, you could write about a real event."
> How can you help yourself to make a decision about what to write? First, check that you have clearly understood the wording in the task. Here, "Write about an incident involving a teacher and a pupil" gives you a wide choice. You are certainly not restricted to writing about a school teacher and school pupil – there are literally hundreds of other possibilities, and you might please an examiner by coming up with an original idea!
> Read the example of writing in response to this task. You will see that this pupil appears not to use the story as a starting point at all. His writing suggests that he has interpreted the task very differently. However, if you look closely at his plan, you can begin to see links. He has in fact used a theme of physical punishment and turned it into a very different sort of story.
> Before reading it though, let us think about how it might have been planned.

PLANNING

What is involved in planning?

Planning can give you an initial idea; it can provide you with a shape or structure to your writing and it can allow you to think about possible scenes for description.

You will know what sorts of plans you feel comfortable with. Some students prefer to plan in a diagram, such as a spider diagram. Others prefer to write lists of events and ideas. Or you can "think aloud" with your writing – quickly jotting down all the ideas as they occur to you.

Literary stimulus 3

What is the link between a plan and the writing?

The purpose of a good plan is not to give you every idea or every word of your work – it is more to start you off and give you confidence. Think of it like a skeleton; your writing can then put all the flesh onto the bones.

One word of warning! Do not become a slave to the plan. Change your ideas as you see new possibilities, whilst you are writing. Here are three types of plan which could be used for the writing on pages 36–7:

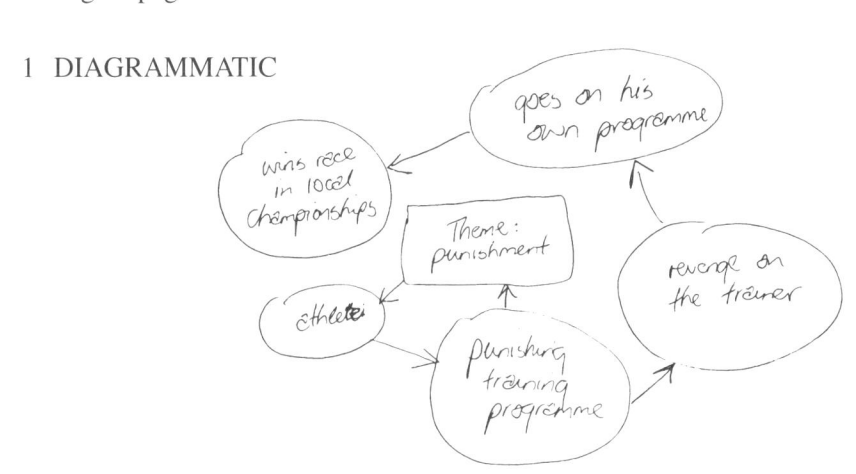

1 DIAGRAMMATIC

[Diagram: Central box "Theme: punishment" connected to bubbles: "goes on his own programme", "wins race in local championships", "athletes", "punishing training programme", "revenge on the trainer"]

2 A LIST

- punishment
- theme of punishment in athletics
- boy being trained by cruel trainer
- revenge against trainer
- wins competition

3 "THINKING ALOUD"

I can see a boy who is an athlete and he is being overtrained by a harsh trainer who because he was injured wants the boy to win but he really wants to win for himself – the boy rejects the trainer and trains himself – this leads to an ending where the boy wins, the trainer sees this at the championships

3 Responding to different kinds of stimulus material

ANSWER

"Write Imaginatively about an incident involving a teacher and a pupil."

"Run faster, boy! You're not trying!" bellowed Mr. Graham.

Mark was running 1500m in his twice-weekly lunchtime training session for the forthcoming regional Junior Athletics Championship. Mr. Graham had agreed to take him on and train him. A tall, powerfully built former athlete, Mr. Graham never seemed satisfied with any of his pupils' achievements. His own athletic career had sadly been cut short when he badly broke his leg falling down some steps. As a result of this he now walked with a kind of sideways limp that made him look like he was not totally balanced all of the time.

"Come on Mark, you're not putting in any effort! Don't you want me to enter you for the Junior Athletics Championship?"

Mark crossed the finish line and sat down, exhausted, on the rubber track.

"I was trying, sir. It's my ankle, sir. It's gone all stiff," complained Mark between breaths. He thought this injury was probably because of Mr. Graham's insistence that he ran 1500 metres at least six times a week.

"Get back onto the track, Mark. You'll only get better with practice." Mr. Graham was a great believer in those old sayings.

"Can't I have a break please? I've been running all lunchtime. Surely I'm fast enough to enter the Championship now!" Mark knew that his time was around the level needed for entry, but to win he needed something extra.

"I give up! You just do not have the right attitude for athletics. You can enter the Championship if you like, but I'm not training you anymore! You should know by now that pride comes between a fall. or before?!"

Mr. Graham walked off as briskly as his ankle would allow, leaving Mark sitting on the track, his head in his hands.

Mark vowed to himself that he would enter the Junior Athletic championship and he would win the 1500 metres, just to show Mr. Graham that he was wrong to not believe in his ability. He told himself that he would design a training schedule that he felt happy with. He would make use of the two weeks before the Championship to maximise his potential.

Literary stimulus 3

> He had decided that varying the type of running would be more likely to improve his chances of winning than the intensive 1500 metre work demanded of him by Mr. Graham. He sent off the entry form for the championship by first class post and waited anxiously for the reply to be sent back, showing if he had fulfilled the entry requirements. This came back satisfactorily and the rest of the two weeks passed very quickly.
>
> On the morning of the championship, Mark was up early to perform his stretching exercises. His father drove him to the nearby athletics ground. He warmed up, then his first heat was called onto the track. Mark walked out nervously, worried whether going it alone was the right decision, after all, Mr. Graham was an ex-athlete himself. If Mark did not win this heat, he could not get into the final, and Mr. Graham would have achieved victory over him.
>
> The race was actually just a formality. Mark won by ten seconds, so went on to the semi-final. This time, though, he was not so lucky. Three of the racers crossed the line at the same time. The result had to go to the judges for adjudication. While Mark was waiting, he saw an old car pull up and a man limp out to join the crowd. Mark's name rang out over the public address system in the list of finalists. Mr. Graham presented him with the gold certificate.

Examiner's commentary

This pupil has achieved a strong sense of character, for both the athlete and the trainer. This has been achieved through the use of dialogue which is used mainly to define the characters. Also, attention is paid to the key relationship between the two characters.

There is considerable variety in the way that the writing is structured. As readers we move from the dialogue during the training session, to a glimpse of Mr Graham's past, when we learn about his accident, then the point where Mark ("that evening") sends off his entry form for the championships, and finally we are brought to the day of the championships when Mr Graham comes back into the story. In fact, the plot is organised in such a way that the reader follows the experiences of the main character to the point where his problems are resolved by a deliberately constructed ending.

There is a good effort to achieve a number of themes in the writing: the punishment in the training schedule at the start; the over zealous enthusiasm of Mr Graham, in the hope that his pupil can be triumphant in his place; and then the themes of rejection, perseverance and triumph towards the end.

There is variety in the sentence structure, much of which is complex. This is an important skill – the ability to write in sentences which cover a number of points through linked or contrasting phrases. There is correct use of tenses in the use of verbs, and a number of effective adjectives and adverbs are also used. The punctuation and paragraphing, two other key skills, are also accurate.

Above all, the pupil is clearly in control of his ideas here and this gives the story a sense of progression. This may have been the result of careful planning.

3 Responding to different kinds of stimulus material

MEDIA STIMULUS

The next two pages contain an example of stimulus material taken from a media source: a newspaper article. Think about how the style of writing, and the vocabulary, differs from the stimulus material taken from literature.

STIMULUS MATERIAL

Care? We don't even want to know

Contact with a mentally handicapped man teaches Brian Jenkins something about society's — and his own — prejudices

People always try to ignore David. This is a pity because David is one of the friendliest people around. Most days he commutes by train, and he always tries to talk to other passengers; but they usually ignore him. Apart from being so friendly, what makes David different from other commuters is that he is mentally handicapped.

When I first saw David (not his real name), I put him down as someone to be avoided. But it was not easy. Every morning there he would be, chatting to whomever was around, shouting greetings to the platform staff and waving to the train drivers.

Most people he spoke to quickly acknowledged him, and walked on. Everyone else, including me, steered clear. Then one day he caught me unawares. I was reading when I heard a voice close by: 'Hello'. I looked up and there he was, grinning widely.

'Oh, hello,' I mumbled, forcing a smile, and turned back to my book. He said something I could not understand. 'Pardon?' I replied. He repeated it; again I could not make it out. Not wishing to appear rude, I replied, 'Oh, really?'. I tried to look engrossed in my book and wished he would go away. He did not. Instead he became my regular travelling companion.

Every morning I shared half an hour on the train with him and while I never found out much about him, I learned a bit about myself and my prejudices, and something about our society.

David must be in his late forties, he is just under 6ft and quite stocky. He has difficulty walking and shuffles his feet. His short-cut hair is grey. He is always smiling, and there is nearly always a drip on the end of his nose. His clothes seem to fit badly, his trousers sag and his blue jacket is a little small.

He always sports a few railway badges and carries a shoulder bag that contains his notebook and packed lunch. When he reaches his destination for the day, he will stand on the platform, noting down the numbers of passing trains, and later will noisily eat his cling-film-wrapped white-bread sandwiches.

Every day he would shout his greeting across the crowded platform. I felt everyone's eyes on me. They seemed glad it was me, not them. Sometimes I heard comments like, 'It's all right, that man must be looking after him' or, 'They really shouldn't let these people out.'

A few years ago Jasper Carrot exposed our fear of mentally handicapped people when he asked 'Why does the looney on the bus always sit next to me?' By laughing, we shared the feeling. As I spent more time with David, I wanted to find out about him. But anything other than questions such as where had he been and where was he going were met with a blank smile. Once I told him I had seen a very unusual train. He asked me if he was going to see it. I replied that there was no way I could know, but he asked me again and again if he was going to see it.

I believe David lives with his family, and I presume they pay for his travels. As he is out and about almost everyday, and occasionally he goes further afield for a few days, his fares must cost quite a bit, even with his Disabled Person's Railcard. Perhaps he had an accident that left him like this, and he is living off the damages or a pension.

One day he showed me some photographs, mainly of trains, stations and gardens. One picture was of an elderly woman. 'Who's this?' I asked. 'My mum,' he replied indignantly, as if I should already know. There was another one of him and a young woman. They were standing under a tree. She looked friendly and kindly. He had his arm round her. 'That's my girlfriend,' he said.

Some time later I met him the day after his

Media stimulus 3

birthday, and he told me about the presents and cards he had received. But, he added sadly, he had not received one from his girlfriend. This was the first time I ever noticed his smile fade.

There was a time when I found myself almost envying David. He did not have to worry about his job, his mortgage, or the rust on his car. He spent every day doing what he liked, train spotting. I thought there was something endearing about this adult with a child's outlook. Then, when I caught him off guard, I saw he looked sad and lost. And I remembered that children have sadness and frustration as much, if not more than, adults.

After some weeks of commuting together, I started to tire of his company. The difficult conversations that led nowhere were hard work. David did not respond to the usual polite signals. I was trying to tell him that I did not want his company, but he did not understand.

I had to face up to a dilemma. Should I treat him as an equal and explain that I needed to be left alone, or should I make a special allowance? The one thing I did not want was to hurt his feelings. In the end I decided to do what I wanted: I explained that I needed to work on the train, and asked if he would allow me to get on with it.

It did not work. In the end I would avoid him at the station. I would duck behind pillars or lurk at the end of the platform. But sometimes he would still see me, and would rub my nose in my guilt by coming over, full of smiles, to say hello. Occasionally he would offer me a Mars Bar, or ask if I wanted a coffee.

Then I changed my commuting pattern, and I no longer caught the same train as David. In a strange way I missed his company. For months I did not see him, then one day, out of the train window, I saw him on the platform. There he was smiling away, talking to a woman. She obviously was not enjoying his company.

I realised how awful we are: David is seriously disadvantaged, and yet all he wants from the rest of us is a bit of friendship. It made me see how the concept of 'Care in the Community' was flawed. As a community, we just do not care, we do not even want to know. And that is probably our loss.

TASK

1. From the article, state four facts about David.
2. Identify and comment on four things that can be understood about David from the passage.
3. Write about ways in which the writer uses language to express his views.
4. What meanings and ideas are there in the final two sentences of the article?
5. Write a brief article of your own persuading teenagers to treat disabled people sympathetically.

Examiner's tip

Here you are asked to show that you can tell the difference between facts and ideas, or inferences. The reading skills that are tested are the selection of information, and then commenting, or evaluating how that information is used. In question 4 you are also being asked to make effective use of information in your own writing.

A close reading of the passage is important. Then, in question 1 you will need to identify clearly what can be stated as fact. Question 2 explores points that can be more widely understood – points that can be inferred, implied in the writing, in other words, points that can be "picked up" through a close reading. Question 3 is another of those questions which asks you to comment on the use of language. You really ought to consider the way that there is a mixture of personal story and argument, designed to enlist our sympathy, and perhaps our feelings of guilt. Question 4 asks for understanding of a particularly important part of the passage, and finally, question 5 tests both reading and writing skills. You will need to use the ideas in your own writing, and to make sure that you are writing for a purpose – here, to explain and persuade.

In the following answer, the examiner recognises that many of the skills have been covered successfully, although in the first question, bald facts are not really stated with absolute confidence.

Care? We don't even want to know.   5.12.96   i.

1. 4 significant facts about David.
   i. David is unaware that people try to avoid him, he goes to them and tries to make friends, but all the time, he is naive to the fact that they don't want to talk to him.
   ii. David has quite a lot of confidence. It takes a lot of 'guts' to approach a stranger and try to start a friendly conversation.
   iii. David has some secret sorrow, that he momentarily is reminded of, and a pained look crosses his face.
   iv. He is childlike in his approach to life. He seems to have endless enthusiasm for life, but like many children (and adults) he has moments of sadness.

   Are these all straight facts?

2. Identify and comment on four points that can be inferred from the passage, about David.
   i. "Most people he spoke to quickly acknowledged him, and walked on"
   – This shows that David is thought of as a nuisance. People try to avoid him, and try to get out of a lengthy conversation with him. They find him strange, and abnormal, so therefore he must be avoided. Peoples views towards David are very naive and prejudiced, they don't understand what motivates him, so therefore he must be weird.

   ii. "Should I treat him as an equal and explain that I needed to be left alone, or should I make a special allowance?"
   – When a person of normal mentality starts a friendly conversation up with you on the train, you reply and speak about neutral topics. But because David is mentally handicapped, they feel that he is unable to keep up a friendly conversation, and that he may take advantage of a situation, and may be very volatile. But no one is willing to give him that chance. Do you really have too much work to do on the train, or is that just an excuse to get rid of him. Surely he should be given a chance, and treated as an equal, to prove himself,

   and to let him speak to you, to make a new friend, which would obviously please him.

   iii. "I never found out much about him, I learned a bit about myself and my prejudices, and something about our society"
   – This is a very thoughtful sentence. It shows how people can be prejudiced, without even realising that they are. To generalise about society as a whole, shows the way that a mentally handicapped person's persistence, can open your eyes to the whole naivity of society today. David is like a normal happy go lucky child, and that he is harmless. When he wishes to speak with you, he does it purely for companionship and probably is not intelligent enough for any harmful ulterior motive, that the public expect him to have.

   iv. "There was a time when I found myself almost enjoying David."

— This statement seems to me to be very hurtful. David is happy with his life and knows no different. I think that it is wrong to envy someone because they have no responsibilities. Although I'm sure he wouldn't want your pity, David will never experience the joys of some parts of adult life, he is stuck in a time warp. I'm sure that if David understood, he would rather be mentally normal, and have bills etc, than be a child all his life. ✓

3. The language that the author uses to express his views, seems to be fairly basic, aimed at an audience of all ages, with fairly basic language and a sophisticated layout of his views, opinions and narrative.

There is a certain amount of guilt voiced through the writer, making you feel ashamed of any prejudices you, as the reader, have ever had, and are likely to have, in a similar situation.

Brian Jenkins lays out his thoughts in a very orderly way. Going from annoyance, to guilt, to annoyance and then to guilt, sympathy and a slight amount of pity.

The writer uses fairly detailed descriptions of situations, but he shows that the outcome is always the same. He always gets to the point fairly quickly. Brian Jenkins tries to generalise, to get to the point of all prejudices across society. He tries to broaden people's minds, to show that almost everybody has prejudices about something and/or someone. Brian Jenkins tries to get us to acknowledge our prejudices and work through them.

As Brian Jenkins writes about a true story, the way he comes to the point about general prejudices is not condescending or patronising, which through his narrative, helps us to come to terms with any adverse thoughts that we may have. *Good, effective analysis.*

4. 'As a community, we just do not care, we do not even want to know. And that is probably our loss'

Brian Jenkins describes many prejudices generally. It is our loss if we don't help people at a disadvantage, as we have help we can give them, but there is probably a lot that they could give you. People think of helping disabled people as a one way thing, we do all the giving, whilst the disabled people do all the taking. But the other people, the disabled people, also have a lot to give. They can open your eyes to many issues and problems that they have. Many mentally handicapped people are naive to many troubles, and so are therefore calm, and at peace with the world and themselves. These people may be able to help you relax, as the helper, just by conveying their tranquility to you.

Interesting thoughts here.

3 Responding to different kinds of stimulus material

5. Write an article for a teenage magazine persuading young people to treat mentally handicapped people sympathetically.

In your eyes they are strange and weird. But to themselves they are content children. When you look at a mentally handicapped person, they may look perfectly normal, if any human is "normal". Until they speak or even move, they are just like you or me. But when it dawns on you, that they are in fact different, you put up a wall between you and the mentally handicapped person. Why?

Unless you are used to people with a mental handicap, I'm sure most would do it. But these people are just naive and young, in mind, even if not in body. Sure, some mentally handicapped people are crazed murderers or have suicidal tendencies, but not the majority.

Many with mental hanicaps just want friendship and will be content with that. But others want more – taking to the park or to the cinema, by you. Special care workers can do that but do they have time to sit, and listen, and be a real friend? You could do that.

Even giving a friendly smile to a person with disibilities or walking by and saying hi, to a person you see regularly. Why not?, it doesn't cost you anything. But as many of them are young in the mind, they will be able to return the smile or hi, but not able to give you the real knowledge that they want more than hi, so they will be content with that.

When passing a mentally handicapped person, don't give them a wide berth, point and laugh at them, don't intentionally or even unintentionally hurt their feelings. Walk by, don't stare, even give them a smile, and make their day.

Treat them as one of you, because they are. Treat them, as you would expect others to treat you. You wouldn't want people to stare, point or make fun of you, so why do it to them? Treat them as a friend, not as an enemy.

They are the ones that have to live with the problem of being mentally handicapped, not you. Make their lives easier, not harder.

Excellent – good range of understanding; points well made, and a persuasive article of your own.

(A)

Non-fiction stimulus 3

One of the types of non-fiction writing specified in the National Curriculum is travel writing.

Printed below is an extract from the Summer 1995 *AA Magazine* in which a particular drive in the Lake District in northern England is described. Read the passage carefully and then consider the questions which follow it.

AA Great Drives: Vroom! with a view

Are there any 'great drives' left to be had in this country? Can you still climb in the car and escape to another, better world? The answer, if I hadn't known it before, was yes; here was the proof – a breathtaking view of England's last wilderness.

I was 1,940 windswept feet above sea level, on the western flank of the Pennines, halfway through a 180 mile drive suggested by the *AA Tour Guide Britain*: the view was a bonus, because the drive up from Melmerby to Hartside Top had in itself been five miles of pure motoring pleasure. And then it was a memorable run over the high moors to the little town of Alston.

The route up the A686 through the Cumbrian hills was one of the highlights of my tour. I'd set off from Carlisle, which is marking the 250th anniversary of its role in Bonnie Prince Charlie's ill-fated rebellion. If you're travelling *en famille*, the children could discover the more blood-curdling aspects of feuding at medieval Carlisle Castle, which fell to the Scots in 1745. It lies within musket range of the B5299 that runs through gentle meadows with the Lake District's peak spanning the southern horizon.

There are splendid views across the glistening Solway Firth to Scotland from a point just before the road dips into Caldbeck. The village churchyard is home to the grave of John Peel, the 19th-century huntsman famed in song.

Wandering sheep are typical moorland hazards on the unclassified road that winds towards Bassenthwaite Lake – a great finger of water that beckons you into the heart of the Lake District. This is where the really spectacular scenery and demanding contours begin, so the car has to work that much harder.

The Winlatter Pass climbs through a pine forest, then runs down to the pleasant village of Low Lorton. A few miles later, the B5289 wriggles along the virtually uninhabited shores of Crummock Water and Buttermere, two of the region's smallest and most beautiful lakes (could it be time for a picnic?).

The road appears to be heading for a cul-de-sac, hemmed in by craggy mountains streaked by waterfalls. But it swings left and climbs the dramatic Honister Pass, snaking between steep, scree-covered slopes littered with huge boulders. Once a year, the quarry at the top of the Pass is the venue for the Vintage Sports Car Club's idiosyncratic Lakeland Trial. Bugattis, Bentleys and other valuable old-timers attempt to climb a long, rough, slippery twisting track that ordinary mortals would think twice about tackling in a modern four-wheel-drive Land Rover.

On the far side of the Pass, the B5289 ducks and dives through wooded Borrowdale before entering Keswick. The busy little

3 Responding to different kinds of stimulus material

town, once a market and mining centre, is now a magnet for tourists, walkers and climbers. I headed for the Cars of the Stars Motor Museum, run by a local dentist, where the attractions include two batmobiles, Patrick McGoohan's Lotus Super Seven from *The Prisoner*, the Aston Martin driven by James Bond and the reliant Regal van run by Derek 'Del Boy' Trotter in BBC-TV's *Only Fools and Horses*. And if that doesn't grab the children, there's the world's largest pencil at the Cumberland Pencil Museum. Coloured pencils have been manufactured in Keswick since the mid-19th century and originally depended on the local graphite deposit.

Helvellyn's pine-clad slopes shelter the A591 as it sweeps down to Grasmere. This Lakeland landscape was muse to Wordsworth who lived in Dove Cottage in Grasmere and at Rydal Mount down the road. At the entrance to Grasmere churchyard, where the poet is buried, what used to be the village school is now a tiny shop. I left with several pieces of the local gingerbread, made to a secret recipe since Queen Victoria was on the throne.

Maximum concentration is essential on the A593 from Ambleside to Coniston. Despite its A-class status, this is a narrow road that, in places, winds between intimidating stone walls. Coniston's forested hinterland offers fine walks; if you seek a more sedate pace, take a cruise aboard *Gondola*, a 136-year-old steam yacht restored by the National Trust. She glides along Coniston Water, where Donald Campbell's attempt on the world water speed record ended in tragedy in 1967. His jet-powered *Bluebird* was doing about 300mph when it crashed.

Coniston is also a good place for an overnight stop. I can endorse the AA's opinion of the Premier Selected 17th-century Wheelgate Country House Hotel. Run by Joan and Roger Lupton, this hideaway offers a warm welcome – from a cosy bar to comfortable bedrooms and excellent food.

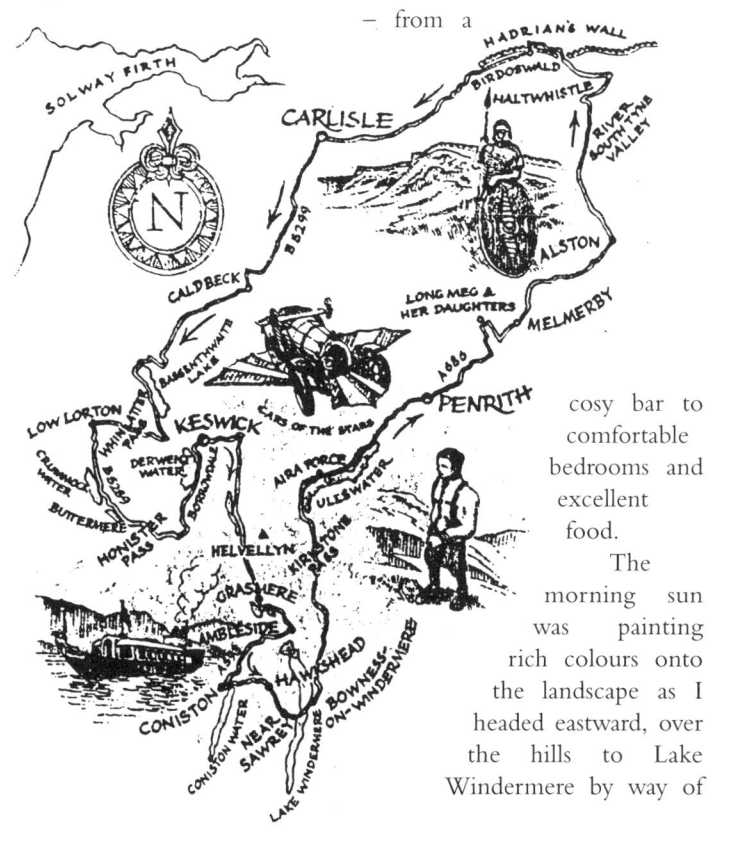

The morning sun was painting rich colours onto the landscape as I headed eastward, over the hills to Lake Windermere by way of Hawkshead and Near Sawrey, where Beatrix Potter lived at Hill Top, a 17th-century farmhouse. The world of Peter Rabbit and other Potter creations is brought to life in the drawings at the museums here – a possible diversion for little children. But I drove on, somewhat concerned that the Wheelgate Hotel's generous breakfast would exceed the eight-ton weight limit for the ferry, which takes four minutes to reach Bowness-on-Windermere. The Steamboat Museum nearby features working vintage craft.

North of Windermere, fields bright with buttercups flank the A592 as it starts its long and increasingly spectacular charge to the Kirkstone Pass. This serpentine road requires the driver to concentrate on the car's ride, roadholding, steering, brakes, acceleration and gearbox. It also measures a driver's patience if stuck behind a coach, because overtaking opportunities are as rare as snowmen in the Sahara.

The mood changes while driving along the western shore of Ullswater. You pass the Aira force waterfall, the place where Wordsworth was inspired by 'a host of golden daffodils', and gradually exchange the Lake District's craggy grandeur for softer landscapes near Penrith. A mile or two of dual-carriageway spans the M6, then it's on to the

Non-fiction stimulus 3

A686 and you come upon the lovely Eden valley.

If you want to share a Cumbrian secret, turn left for Hunsonby, about 1.5 miles after Langwathby and follow the lanes to where Long Meg and her Daughters stand in a field in an isolated farm. Few discover this prehistoric stone circle – and the absence of visitors makes it all the more magical. It's only a five-mile detour.

Stop for a coffee and delicious home-made goodies at the Village Bakery in Melmerby; then it's a pleasant 10-mile drive to Alston, which is England's highest town. This is where the mood changes again as moorland gives way to the valley of the South Tyne river.

The last six miles of the drive to Haltwhistle are a delight, because this is a road whose quality belies its unclassified status.

Today's motorists can cover in a few effortless minutes distances that represented a brutally long day's march to the legionnaires who manned Hadrian's Wall, north of Haltwhistle. The Roman Army Museum at Greenhead is a tribute to them. Nearby, the other tangible links with Roman times include the fort at Birdoswald, where the road runs past a well-preserved length of the coast-to-coast wall that protected the Roman Empire's northern frontier.

Later, on the road back to Carlisle, I found myself reflecting that there are two equally rewarding aspects to a great drive. For some the pleasure of motoring lies in the freedom to stop and to savour the scenery. For others, the quality of driving is the paramount consideration. Take this heart of Lakeland drive and both wishes will be delightfully fulfilled.

TASK

1. The writer of this article describes what he is writing about as a "great drive". In no more than 150 words summarise why he considers it to be a "great drive". Then briefly give your opinion of what he says.

2. The article is set out in a way which is designed to attract you to the idea of doing the trip yourself. Analyse the way in which the article is written and the way in which it was presented. Does it succeed in its aim?

You should refer to: the vocabulary and writing style,
the layout and use of illustration.

Examiner's tip The key to success in answering this question is to identify the skills that you are being asked to use. Try to use each skill as precisely as possible. In Question 1 you are asked first of all to write a summary. Here, it is important to stick to the limit of 150 words. Be clear about each separate point – summary is a precise exercise and you cannot include anything other than the key points. The second part of Question 1 is more open, involving the skill of evaluation. When you are asked to give your opinion on the writer's views, make sure that what you write is i) genuinely based on what the the writer has said; ii) of significance; iii) supported by argument or evidence. Note that you are not simply being asked to give your opinion on the topic; you are asked to respond to the *writer's* views.

The second question requires a close analysis of language. This is an important question as it tests your understanding of how language is used for particular purposes and effects. You would be expected to comment on some of the persuasive, descriptive style of language, which has an effect of a relaxed, easy approach relevant to a leisurely drive or holiday mood. In addition, there are aspects of the graphics and structure that, you might decide, help the reader to follow the points, such as the columns, the illustrations and the use of maps.

Don't forget that you are also asked to evaluate the language. Does it succeed? This requires more than a yes or no answer! You must be prepared to provide reasons and support these with evidence from the article.

3 Responding to different kinds of stimulus material

ANSWER

Travel Writing

The route passes through England's last wilderness which includes gentle meadows, pine forests, beautiful lakes, a waterfall and numerous picturesque villages. This breathtaking scenery all adds to why he finds the drive so appealling.

His second and most detailed reason is that there are so many interesting places to visit. The area has a number of museums ranging from famous cars to the Roman army museum. The journey also takes in the grave of John Peel, Carlisle castle, the home of Beatrix Potter and a prehistoric stone circle.

His final reason as to why this is a 'great drive' is the pure driving pleasure that can be gained from the narrow, winding roads. The encompassing stone walls add a touch of danger to the drive which cause the driver to concentrate on his steering, braking, accelerating and gear changing, all the things that make driving so enjoyable.

I think that that the writer has to say is quite interesting and very well expressed. He uses a lot of detail during his exploration of the local sights, which along with his inclusion of historical references provides a lot of interesting information about the area. This makes the area seem more appealling to the reader. I especially like that he has to say about the views and driving. He uses an excellent selection of adjectives, such as 'splendid' and 'spectacular' to describe the quite breathtaking views. His description of the driving conditions and driving itself is brilliant, especially the way he describes the roads as 'serpentine' and states that 'the car has to work that much harder,' which really highlights the thrills that can be obtained from driving on the winding roads.

The article is written in an informal and very informative style. The writer uses a lot of information when referring to the different sights and places to visit on the trip. Not only does the writer use a lot of information to describe the sight, such as including the main attractions of the cars at the stars motor museum, but he gives a little historical insight into the place. Things like mentioning Donald Campbell's death on the Coniston water, whilst attempting to

Non-fiction stimulus 3

break the world water speed record, make the locations seem more interesting. This in turn will entice more people into doing the drive.

The use of vocabulary is also impressive as it helps to bring across the real beauty of the area which is one of the article's main features in terms of attracting drivers. The use of adjectives like 'breathtaking' and 'spectacular' when describing the views, tells you that the views are obviously extremely beautiful but without saying just what they are. This leaves a touch of intrigue and curiosity in the mind of the reader which again will help to attract drivers. The vocabulary used to describe the actual driving is very clever. "This is where the really spectacular scenery and demanding contours begin, so the car has to work that much harder," is a brilliant use of vocabulary as the use of the adjective 'demanding' makes the driving seem that little bit more challenging which would definitely appeal to any driving enthusiasts who were considering doing the drive.

The use of illustrations in the article is a very successful way of showing the beauty of the area. The pictures are well set out so that they catch the eye and are quite logical as they are positioned next to the relevant text. The pictures show a mixture of the countryside and activities in the area so that they back up the text with a visual presentation. The best use of illustrations is the map of the area. It is very informative and unlike most maps is interesting and visually stunning as the use of diagrams is a clever way of showing where the activities are.

The article most certainly succeeds in its aim to encourage people to do the trip. By describing the picturesque landscape, the numerous places to visit and the driving pleasure that can be obtained from the trip, it appeals to a wide variety of people and makes the trip sound very interesting and most importantly, very inviting.

Examiner's commentary This candidate has covered all the points in the questions. In response to Question 1, the summary is sound. The main points are presented, within the word limit, in a concise and well organised way. The evaluation of the writer's views is well supported with reference to the article, and not simply as an assertion of opinion.

Question 2 is perhaps less successful overall: although effective points are made about the use of powerful adjectives, the attempted analysis of vocabulary is more vague, and the examiner feels that this candidate has failed to do justice to the persuasiveness of the language. The points about the illustrations and maps are handled securely, as is the final evaluation, which successfully draws the points together.

3 Responding to different kinds of stimulus material

MEDIA AND NON-FICTION STIMULI

What follows are two pieces of stimulus material, one from a media source and one from a non-fiction source, an autobiography. Both pieces appeared in The Sunday Times 15, October 1995. The task gives you the chance to practise three different types of response.

Read both passages carefully.

STIMULUS MATERIAL

A GENTLE TOUCH FOR THE PUPILS SICK OF SCHOOL

With the initial excitement of starting at the "big" school behind them, the vast majority of Year 7 pupils at comprehensives have settled comfortably into a new routine. But for others the transition is a cause of considerable distress.

It is believed that up to 140,000 children in Britain could be suffering from "school phobia" and a big "trigger point" is the change of schools at 11. The emotional wrench caused by exchanging the comparative security of a small primary school for the perceived impersonality of a large comprehensive can cause a phobia to take route. Phobic symptoms include bed-wetting, headaches and being physically sick at the mere thought of school. Other warning signs are excessive worrying about uniform, using the toilet, changing for PE and eating in public. As the phobia grows, the child will often give up social activities such as sports or Scouts in order to avoid any contact whatsoever with other children.

What can be done? Already comprehensives are eager to build friendly links with their feeder primary schools and comprehensive teachers are regular visitors to primary school assemblies. All comprehensives are now keen to foster a pupil-friendly image and glossy prospectuses are distributed showing the "fun" side of school life. "Taster" days are set up when Year 6 children can meet their new teachers and get used to finding their way around their future school.

John Deacon, head of Poltair school in St Austell, Cornwall, believes that this is not enough. Taking pupils from 22 feeder schools, some with as few as 80 on the roll, there is the obvious risk that a new pupil will feel lost in the 1200 strong comprehensive. To combat this Deacon has set up a carefully planned familiarisation programme. Children from Year 7 in the comprehensive school return to their former schools to work on dance and drama projects and the primary school children spend whole days at the comprehensive. Rather than simply receiving sample lessons, the children mix with those from the year above them and participate fully in classwork. They gain reassurance from talking with the older children and, as a result, few experience a sense of trauma when they move up.

Of course, for some the culture shock of the comprehensive is still hard to assimilate. If problems do arise then, again, the emphasis is placed on the child receiving help from fellow pupils. Deacon sees this as the key to his school's success in helping new pupils to find their feet.

"Children with problems are very unlikely to share their worries with a teacher, so we provide them with 'mentors' – children a year older who help them cope with the practicalities and who try to find out what is really bothering them," he said. "Things like the lunchtime eating arrangements can be a cause of concern and the mentor helps the child through these potentially worrying points in the school day. The mentor reports back to the head of year and often something trivial is the cause of the anxiety. Hopefully, the head of year can reassure the pupil and the problem can be nipped in the bud."

Media and non-fiction stimuli

STIMULUS MATERIAL

THE RELUCTANT BOARDER

... We were the first to arrive, a habit my mother never lost, much to the amusement of the other kids at school. Nobody else arrived for about three hours. We were greeted by Brother Bede, a tall ginger-bearded Geordie, who was dressed from head to toe in a black robe, finished off with a white dog collar. I remember my mother taking me up to my dormitory, making my bed and unpacking my stuff into the tatty wooden locker beside it. I was to share a room with 11 other boys. I remember needing to go to the lavatory and being confused by the wall of urinals – I had never seen any before. I don't remember much about the other children, who arrived throughout the afternoon, but my mother tells me I was shy and a bit nervous of them. They were all much older than me: I was the youngest by two years. The only friend I made initially was Sausage, the school cat, a fat tabby whose eventual fate defies description.

At about 4.00 p.m. it was time to say goodbye to my mother. It must have been so much harder for her, because she knew what was happening. She said: "I have to go Stephane." I calmly acknowledged this fact and kissed her on the cheek. I then turned to Brother Bede and said: "I would like to be called Steve from now on." God knows why I did it, but my mother instantly said: "No, your name is Stephane and I want you to be called Stephane." Brother Bede agreed and I didn't push the issue any further. My mother left in her car, drove 100 metres up the road and burst into tears. I carried on playing happily with Sausage the cat.

It wasn't until bedtime that the whole thing really began to dawn on me. I couldn't understand why I was going to bed in this strange place and why my mother still hadn't come to pick me up. I had shared a bed with my mother since I was a baby. I remember getting out of bed and hearing others around me whimpering in the darkness. I strode out of the dormitory into the hall, half expecting my mother to be there. She wasn't. I walked along the hall and turned right into the refectory. I called out for her. No answer. I started to feel anxious and began to cry. I returned to the hall and in the distance I could just make out the outline of a figure approaching. I called out again, thinking it must be her. No answer. The figure drew nearer. It was Brother Bede. "What are you doing out of bed?" he asked. "I was looking for my mum," I replied, between snuffles. He then went on to explain everything that my mother had already told me and that, basically, I was not going to see her for some time.

TASK

1. Read the first passage again carefully and summarise the problems which young children might have when they start a new school.

2. The writer of the autobiography wants us to have sympathy with him as a young boy. Explain how he has written in a way which engages our sympathy. You may refer to:
   - the vocabulary he has used;
   - the lengths of sentences and phrases;
   - the detail of the events which are described.

3. Imagine that you are Stephane. You have been at your boarding school for half a term. Write a letter home to your mother telling her about your life.

3 Responding to different kinds of stimulus material

> **Examiner's tip** In the summary, a word limit is not stated. It is still important that the main points are summarised as precisely as possible. This is the sort of exercise which tests your understanding of key points in a passage, and your ability to rewrite them as clearly as you can. Make sure that you do not write too much.
>
> Question 2 requires an analysis of the language in the autobiography. You have to ask yourself: what is the writer doing with language in order to make an impact on me? Whenever you are asked to comment on how a writer has written, you are inevitably being asked to talk about language.
>
> In Question 3 you will need to take on the role of the character and write in an appropriate tone. This is an imaginative task and so it will be a good idea to think out some ideas first: What kinds of things might he write about? What sorts of events might have happened? Will the life at the school have changed during half a term? Obviously, it is a personal letter, so the tone will be informal, but that should not stop you from including details about the life of the school, some of which you can pick up in the extract.

ANSWER

When children start a new school it can sometimes be very problematic. Occasionally they may be so distressed and disconcerted that they may be suffering from 'school phobia.' This is when a child is so nervous and upset about joining their new school that they begin to wet the bed, receive pounding headaches and are actually being not only mentally ill but physically sick at even just the thought of going to school. This usually occurs when 11 year old children begin their secondary school education.

The children may feel a great sense of insecurity as they have transferred from a known primary school atmosphere to an alien secondary school atmosphere. The fear that this can inflict can be quite unbelievable, but for many of these children it is very significant. Other problems that the children may face are feeling the trauma and loss in a large secondary school especially if they're finding the culture shock difficult to come to terms with, but also they may begin to worry about trivial things such as their uniform and the way it looks; using the toilet facilities; eating whilst other people are watching, especially if the child is on their own; and changing for PE, if they are insecure about their looks or just changing with other people.

If phobias are allowed to grow then they will gradually destroy any self confidence or self belief that the child possessed. It may end up to the extent where the child cuts themselves off from other children entirely by giving up social activities like sports or youth clubs and instead they begin to withdraw into themselves as they feel terrorised and alienated.

These are an example of some general problems that may occur as a child moves to a new school. There are many others such as bullying, but the problems that I have expanded are the main ones listed in the passage 'A gentle touch for the pupils sick of school.'

✓ Good focus on the key points, well expressed in your own writing.

Media and non-fiction stimuli 3

The Reluctant Boarder

Qu 2: The writer of the autobiography wants us to sympathize with the young boy. He seems to engage our sympathy through some of the vocabulary that is being used. Most of the vocabulary is very descriptive about the mother and the boy's feelings and in many cases actions.

The mother's feelings are shown when the mother says 'No, your name is Stephane and I want you to be called Stephane.' She says this when her son, the boy, wants to change his name to Steve. I believe that the quote shows that the mother is feeling very insecure. She's upset, agitated and worried about leaving her son behind in the boarding school, but she felt that at least her son would still be Stephane and not Steve. I think that she may have felt that if he changed his name then he would change and he wouldn't be her little boy any more. Although changing his name may seem very insignificant, you can acknowledge that through this action you receive a very clear perspective of the mother's feelings and emotions, so we want to sympathize with her, for the possible loss that she may face, of her son.

The boy's feelings are shown in mainly two different ways. The first is when his mother is present and he decides to visit the lavatory, he then states 'I remember going to the lavatory and being confused by the wall of urinals - I had never seen any before.' This shows that the boy is feeling very confused in his new surroundings, upset that his mother has left him and insecure at the thought of being left in this new place, with no-one that he knew. He had never been away from his mother before. He also shows the boy playing with the tabby cat and hardly acknowledging the presence of his mother. I feel that this shows that the boy is putting on an act so as he doesn't upset his mother even more. I think that he is trying to believe that his mother wouldn't leave him, so I think he feels that this is all unreal and isn't really going to happen. He comes across as being calm and brave but you tend to feel sympathy towards the boy as he seems to be handling the situation well, but really we can see through his act, as readers, and understand his real feelings, i.e. fear, helplessness, loss and misunderstanding.

The second main way is the way in which he crumbles during the night when his mother leaves him. Through the use of the descriptive vocabulary you really can perceive what the boy is feeling. He states that he had shared a bed with his mother since he had been a baby. This is important as from this we can stem the trauma and anxiety that he is experiencing. He gets out of bed and looks for his mother. He calls out to her and when there is no answer he begins to cry. We feel real sympathy for the boy when he cries. This is because we try to empathize with the situation that he is in, and at such a young age i.e. 8. We acknowledge the fact that if put in his position we would probably have reacted in the same manner. We can perceive the fear and loss that he is feeling, but most importantly, through the vocabulary we can see the shock and the sudden realisation, that he has lost his mother.

The vocabulary shows us details of events that occurred. These are important as they really do engage our sympathy. When the autobiography begins it states that the boy and his mother were the first to arrive. I think that we feel sympathy towards the boy there because he may be feeling slight embarrassment at being the first to arrive, especially as they arrived 3 hours early.

We also feel sympathy towards the boy when he unpacks his suitcase into a "tatty" wardrobe. It's the word tatty that seems to be the most significant as it gives and creates a picture in our heads of the wardrobe, and around this we can form a picture of the room. I feel that the room is very dark and dull. It's quite dusty and has very little furniture in it, apart from eleven rickety beds and six small tatty wardrobes. The majority of our own rooms are neatly furnished and contain our own possessions. We feel sympathy towards the boy because of the desolation in his dormitory, the bareness and the blankness. We can empathize with the boy because we wouldn't want to be in his position in our lives, yet in his it becomes our experience.

When he quotes "I remember needing to go to the lavatory and being confused by the wall of urinals - I had never seen any before." We can experience and see the shock and confusion that he is experiencing.

We also feel sorry for the boy when he makes friends with the school cat, Sausage. This event seems to insinuate that the boy wasn't able to make other friends, only the friendship of an animal, who can't return love in the same way as a human can.

We feel sorry for him when he goes in search for his mother and can't find her. All he finds instead is a dark, gloomy dormitory full of strangers and a man that he hardly knows who informs him that he won't be seeing his mother for some time. That's when I feel that our sympathy reaches it's peak. This is because we are able to acknowledge the boy's loss and the way in which he has to become independent from his mother and begin to look after himself instead. We find this quite distressing that such a young boy should be removed from his mother when he is so dependant upon her.

These are the ways in which I feel that the writer of the autobiography has successfully written in a way which engages our sympathy through the use of events and vocabulary towards the boy.

The sentences and phrases also are of some significance. They are quite short and concise so as we can build up a picture in our minds of what is happening. But when the boy describes about himself, the sentences are longer and tend to ramble. This makes us take pity on the boy as the more we read of his predicament, the more we sympathize with him.

These are the ways in which I feel that the sentences and phrases assist the writer of the autobiography to engage our sympathy towards the boy.

An excellent answer; a stylish focus on much of the detail and a real analysis of some of the language.

What you have to say about his mother is surely less relevant – the question asked about sympathy for the boy.

Media and non-fiction stimuli 3

Llanelli

16/9/36

Dear Mama,

How are you? I have settled in reasonably well. I miss you, but don't worry about me. I know I'm here because it's the best place for me.

I've made a friend! His name is Sausage. He's the school cat. He's fat and furry but he's a good friend to play with. He always likes to play.

I miss home so much. Everything is so confusing and new here. In the boys' lavatory there are urinals. They're white basin things that hang on the wall. We don't have them at home so I didn't really know what they were for. A boy teased me for not knowing, but a kind boy told me what they are for. It's a bit rude mama so I had better not tell you.

I'm the youngest boy by 2 years, so I'm finding it difficult to make any friends apart from Sausage. I'm not the only home-sick boy though. Sometimes when I lie in bed, looking into the darkness I can hear someone whimpering. I don't know who it is. All I know is that it's one of the 10 boys in my dormitory. I just wish I knew who, then we could be friends. No-one will tell me though as it isn't 'manly' to cry in the boys' opinions.

They still call me Stephane as you wanted. Brother Bede makes sure of that. I like Brother Bede, but not as much as I like you mama. The worst time that I missed you was on my first night here. I went in search of you from my bed as you weren't there. I was confused because I couldn't find you. I ended up crying because you weren't anywhere. I then saw someone approaching. I thought it was you coming back for me, but it wasn't. It was Brother Bede. He had come to put me back to bed and he explained again what you had already told me.

I am coping with the work well. Brother Bede says that I am 'progressing sufficiently'. It seems sort of like home to me, but it will never be complete until you are here. I sometimes sit and wonder what you might be doing. I like to think of you sitting by the fire and rocking me to sleep whilst you sing a lullaby. That's what I dream about and it helps me to sleep on a night.

We do lots of exciting things here. I have a lot more opportunities now to do a lot more things than I ever used to. It can be good fun and I know that being here is what is best for me.

I think Sausage wants me to play with him now. He is making a lot of noise and is weaving around my ankles. Come and visit me soon mama, but don't worry about me as I'm well.

Yours

Stephane.

(and Sausage.)

Very good letter, totally empathising with the boy and developing accounts of the school life.

(A)

Examiner's commentary This candidate has clearly responded to the task with some excellent answers. However, the summary could be more concise and there is some irrelevance in the answer to the second question, especially where she has written about the mother's feelings. Always check that you are only doing what you need to do as this is what will be marked. In other respects, the answer is an excellent one from a candidate who certainly makes an effort to deal with the details of description and with the variety of types of statement about the events. The letter shows empathy with the character.

4 Speaking and listening

Good practice at speaking and listening will help you gain marks for your coursework (speaking and listening is always assessed during the course). Achieving good oral work also helps you to make progress in other parts of the course.

Speaking and listening are assessed in two ways. There are *general criteria* and there are *specific criteria* for the marks given. Let's have a look at what these terms mean.

General criteria are statements about what you are expected to achieve in a number of different speaking and listening tasks. They are descriptions of your overall performance. Here is an example, the general criteria for grade B candidates:

Candidates speak purposefully in a range of contexts of increasing complexity, managing the contributions of others. They exhibit confidence and fluency in talk and show effective use of standard English vocabulary and grammar in a range of situations. They listen with some sensitivity and respond accordingly.

> **Examiner's tip** In order to succeed with meeting the general criteria, try to understand what some of the terms mean.
>
> *Purposeful* speech means taking matters seriously, making important contributions, holding and expressing views. The word *context* describes the different kinds of work you are doing. Think about the way that giving a talk to your class will involve different skills from solving a problem in pairs or discussing a poem in a small group. *Confidence* and *fluency* come from practice, and from having lots of ideas. Always get involved in speaking and listening work in your course. Try to take a strong interest in any points that are debated. Contribute to arguments and discussions. Never just sit back to avoid taking risks!
>
> *Standard English* is the language of public communication. It is the sort of spoken language that everybody will need to use in education and their working lives. Standard English should be clear, with easily understood grammatical constructions which everybody can understand and respond to. We hear standard English around us all the time: in schools, in businesses, in the office, over the telephone, and so on. It's the sort of communication that allows problems, points to be understood and ideas to be communicated. But note that standard English does not involve you in speaking in a false or 'posh' way. This is a common mistake. You are not assessed on your accent, so if you speak with a regional accent, don't try to change it when you are being assessed. Standard English can also be used in both formal (e.g. a meeting) and informal (e.g. amongst friends) situations. The most important thing is that you develop the skill of communicating. There are further comments on the use of standard English in the section that follows on role-play.
>
> The final part of the general criteria refers to *sensitive listening*. Sometimes it is easier to prepare yourself to speak and much more difficult to listen. In fact, of all the things we do with language, listening may be the most difficult. How can you improve your listening skills? There are some useful techniques of *active listening* which you could practise. Firstly, concentration is important. Never let your mind wander! Secondly, always try to think about what is being said – never just hear the words. Higher listening skills involve analysing and interpreting what you are listening to. This involves a lot of concentration, to follow points being made and thinking about whether you agree or disagree with them. Also, help speakers with your own reactions and body language – remember that a good listener encourages a good speaker. Eye contact helps, so too does nodding, smiling, agreeing. On the other hand you can lose marks for putting a speaker off, so never be impolite; don't interrupt, look away or start yawning! You can be marked on listening by showing how ready you are to respond or reply to a speaker. The relevance of what you have to say indicates how good your concentration has been.

Speaking and listening 4

Specific criteria are statements about three different uses of talk. These are:

i) Explain, describe and narrate, for which the grade B criteria are:
   - *respond using a flexible range of vocabulary and grammatical structures to convey meaning, including inferential aspects;*
   - *manage challenging subject matter effectively.*

ii) Explore, analyse, imagine, for which the grade B criteria are:
   - *analyse and reflect effectively on real or imagined experience;*
   - *formulate and interpret information, developing significant points.*

iii) Discuss, argue, persuade, for which the grade B criteria are:
   - *manage collaborative tasks;*
   - *build on, and challenge the points made by others;*
   - *make probing contributions, structuring and organising points made by others.*

> **Examiner's tip**
>
> Quite simply, it is important to be aware of what you are being asked to do in the contexts for your speaking and listening work. Always concentrate on the skills required for the contexts in which you are working. These tips may help:
>
> For individual talks or presentations, plan your main points in notes in order to organise your ideas, but not as a written essay. Some talkers use index cards for their main points: the advantage is that you can keep them in order and discard them after each point has been covered. Do not just talk, communicate! Use eye contact, change the tone and pitch of your voice and pause to give your listener a chance to take things in.
>
> For pair or group planning and discussion: concentrate on the task; be prepared to express new ideas; be supportive of each other – be critical, but never destructive; be prepared to change your mind and accept the views of others; back up your views with evidence or examples; never hog the conversation, but let others have their say.
>
> For the first set of skills, *explaining*, *describing* and *narrating*, be prepared to speak at length with well planned presentations. This often involves giving a talk to the class or to groups. Many good candidates find it helpful to use short prompt cards to remind them of key points.
>
> For *exploring*, *analysing* and *imagining*, be prepared to look into ideas, to share them with others, to support and help other candidates, possibly reaching conclusions.
>
> In tasks which require *discussion*, *argument* and *persuasion*, remember that you need to identify key arguments and always put them across with reasons and evidence to support them. Your own ideas are important, but it is always important to listen to the views of others and see how these affect your own thinking. Another term for argument is *constructive dialogue*. This involves disagreement and criticism, but not in a nasty or unpleasant way. It's a way of trying to find out which points of view are stronger and which can be believed.

Role play

Role play is used quite commonly now to encourage standard English in commonly imagined situations, and also to help candidates explore characters and ideas in literature.

Role play is not the same as drama, so you do not have to act the part of a character, with accent or dialect, etc. Nor do you have to learn lines. To succeed with role play you need to: think what kinds of outlooks and attitudes are appropriate to the role – a few minutes thinking yourself into the role can be helpful; 'become' the person whose role you are playing; experiment with the things they might say; develop and expand your language rather than just stating the obvious; listen carefully to others. Always try to reflect on what you have learnt from playing a role.

5 Exam practice

This section of the book is designed to give you as many chances as possible to practise your skills. For English, practice may not always make perfect but it does give you a chance to think and improve, and is probably the best way there is to revise.

This section is split into two parts. The first part has a selection of tasks, many of which are taken from GCSE exam papers, and the second part contains examiner's tips which advise you on how to approach the various tasks.

Each task has a brief introduction, followed by some stimulus material and then the task itself. Please have a go at the tasks first and then read the tips to see if your approach is what was expected. If you are way out of line with what was expected you might then choose to have another go. Practise hard and good luck with your examination!

TASK 1

We have looked at literary stimulus already: here is a chance to practise yourself. Read the poem "Head of English" which is printed on the accompanying sheet of paper. When you have read it carefully answer the questions which follow it.

STIMULUS MATERIAL

Head of English
by Carol Ann Duffy

Today we have a poet in the class
A real live poet with a published book.
Notice the inkstained fingers girls. Perhaps
we're going to witness verse hot from the press.
5 Who knows. Please show your appreciation
by clapping. Not too loud. Now

sit up straight and listen. Remember
the lesson on assonance, for not all poems
sadly, rhyme these days. Still. Never mind.
10 Whispering's, as always, out of bounds –
but do feel free to raise some questions.
After all, we're paying forty pounds.

Those of you with English Second Language
see me after break. We're fortunate
15 to have this person in our midst.
Season of mists and so on and so forth.
I've written quite a bit of poetry myself,
am doing Kipling with the Lower Fourth.

Right. That's enough from me. On with the Muse.
20 Open a window at the back. We don't
want winds of change about the place.
Take notes, but don't write reams. Just an essay
on the poet's themes. Fine. Off we go.
Convince us that there's something we don't know.

25 Well. Really. Run along now girls. I'm sure
that gave us an insight to an outside view.
Applause will do. Thank you
very much for coming here today. Lunch
in the hall? Do hang about. Unfortunately
30 I have to dash. Tracey will show you out.

Exam practice 5

TASK

1. a. What seems to you to be the attitude of the teacher to the poet who is visiting the class?

    b. Look at the various instructions which are given to the pupils in the class and explain how, as a member of the class, you would react to them. Give reasons for your points.

    c. Certain words and phrases in the poem tell us things about the type of poetry which the teacher prefers. Pick out those words and phrases and suggest what they tell you.

2. Imagine that you are the poet. You get home and are talking to someone about your day. Describe your experience in the lesson.

NEAB 1995

TASK 2

All English syllabuses contain a requirement for reading and working on writing from other cultures. What that means is that you are expected to read stories, poems and so on from cultures other than those which are defined as the English Literary Heritage in the National Curriculum.

The story which follows, which is taken from a book of American short stories, is called "Motel Chronicles (an excerpt)" and is by Sam Shepard. The collection of pieces from which this little story is taken is, in part, observations, poems and thoughts that are a background to a film of his.

Read the story carefully.

STIMULUS MATERIAL

Motel Chronicles (an excerpt)
by Sam Shepard

The first time I ran away from school I was ten. Two older guys talked me into it. They were brothers and they'd both been in and out of Juvenile Hall five times. They told me it would just be like taking a short vacation. So I went. We stole three bikes out of a back yard and took off for the Arroyo Seco. The bike I stole was too big for me so I could never sit up on the seat all the way. I pedalled standing.

We hid the bikes in a stand of Eucalyptus trees at the edge of the Arroyo and went down to the creek. We caught Crawdads with marshmallow bait then tore the shells off them and used their meat to catch more Crawdads. When lunch time came I had to share my lunch with the brothers because they'd forgotten to bring theirs. I spread the contents of the paper bag out on a big flat rock. A carrot wrapped in wax paper with a rubber band around it. A meatloaf sandwich. A melted bag of M and Ms. They ate the M and Ms first. Tore the package open and licked the chocolate off the paper. They offered me a lick but I declined. I didn't eat any of the meatloaf sandwich either. I always hated meatloaf. Especially cold and between bread.

The rest of the afternoon we climbed around in the hills looking for snakes until one of them got the idea of lowering our bikes down into the aqueduct and riding along the dry bed until we reached Los Angeles. I said 'yes' to everything even though I suspected LA was at least a hundred miles away. The only other time I'd ever been to Los Angeles was when my Aunt took me to the Farmer's Market in her '45 Dodge to look at the Myna birds. I must have been six then.

I climbed the chain-link barrier fence while the two brothers took the tension out of the barb-wire strands at the top. Enough so I could straddle the fence, get one foot on the concrete wall of the aqueduct and drop some ten or twelve feet to the bottom. Then they lowered the bikes down to me, suspended on their belts. We rode for miles down this giant corridor of cement, the wheels of our bikes bumping over the brown lines of caulking used to seal the seams. Except for those seams it was the smoothest, flattest surface I'd ever ridden a bike on.

We rode past red shotgun shells faded by the sun, dead opossums, beer cans, Walnut shells, Carob pods, a Raccoon with two babies, pages out of porno magazines, hunks of rope, inner tubes, hub caps, bottle caps, dried-up Sage plants, boards with nails, stumps, roots, smashed

57

5 Exam practice

glass, yellow golf balls with red stripes, a lug wrench, women's underwear, tennis shoes, dried-up socks, a dead dog, mice, Dragon Flies screwing in mid-air, shrivelled-up frogs with their eyes popped out. We rode for miles until we came to a part that was all enclosed like a big long tunnel and we couldn't see light at the other end. We stopped our bikes and stared through the mouth of that tunnel and I could tell they were just as scared as I was even though they were older. It was already starting to get dark and the prospect of getting stuck in there at night, not knowing how long the thing was or what town we'd come out in or how in the hell we were going to climb back out once we came to the end of it, had us all wishing we were back home. None of us said we wished that but I could feel it passing between us.

I don't remember how the decision was made but we pushed off straight ahead into it. The floor was concave and slick with moss, causing the wheels to slip sideways. Sometimes our feet came down ankle-deep in sludge and black mud and we ended up having to walk the bikes through most of it. We kept making sounds to each other just to keep track of where we were as the light disappeared behind us. We started out trying to scare each other with weird noises but gave it up because the echoes were truly terrifying. I kept having visions of Los Angeles appearing suddenly at the other end of the tunnel. It would just pop up at us, all blinking with lights and movement and life. Sometimes it would appear like I'd seen it in postcards. (Palm Trees set against a background of snowy mountains with orange groves sprawling beneath them. The Train Station with a burro standing in front of it, harnessed to a cart.) But it didn't come. For hours it didn't come. And my feet were wet. And I forgot what the two brothers even looked like anymore. I kept having terrible thoughts about home. About what would happen when I finally got back. In the blackness I pictured our house. The red awning. The garage door. The strip of lawn down the centre of the driveway. The Pyracantha berries. The Robins that ate them. Close-ups of the Robin's beak guzzling red berries. So close I could see little dribbles of dirt from wet lawns where he'd been pulling out worms. I couldn't stop these pictures. (Me walking to school. The chubby old Crossing Guard at the corner with his round wooden sign that read STOP in red letters. The dirt playground. Porcelain water fountains with silver knobs dribbling. The face of the kid I hit in the stomach for no reason. Little traces of mayonnaise around his lips.) I had the feeling these pictures would drown me. I wondered what the two brothers were thinking but I never asked them.

It was night when we reached the end and it wasn't Los Angeles either. Huge Sycamore trees with hazy orange street lights loomed over our heads. We could hear the sound of a freeway. Periodic whooshing of trucks. We hauled ourselves out by climbing on each other's shoulders and hooking the belts to the top of the fence. The oldest brother said he recognized the town we were in. He said it was Sierra Madre and he had an Uncle who lived pretty close by. We pedalled to his Uncle's house and we weren't talking to each other at that point. There was nothing to say.

His Uncle lived in a small three-room house with several men sitting around the front room drinking beer and watching the Lone Ranger on TV. Nobody seemed surprised to see us. They acted like this had happened a lot before. A woman was making a big pot of spaghetti in the kitchen and she gave us each a paper plate and told us to wait for the meat sauce to heat up. We sat on the floor at the feet of the men in the front room and watched the Lone Ranger and ate spaghetti. That was the first time I'd ever seen TV because we didn't have one at home. (My Dad said we didn't need one.) I liked the Lone Ranger a lot. Especially the music when he galloped on Silver and reared up waving his hat at a woman holding a baby.

We were finally caught later that night by a squad car on a bridge in South Pasadena. The cops acted like we were adults. They had that kind of serious tone: 'Where did you get these bikes? What are your names? Where do you live? Do you know what time it is?' Stuff like that. They radioed our parents and confiscated the bikes. My mother showed up and drove me back, explaining how my Dad was so pissed off that he wouldn't come because he was afraid he'd kill me. She kept saying, 'Now you've got a Police Record. You'll have that the rest of your life.'

I got whipped three times with the buckle-end of my Dad's belt. Three times. That was it. Then he left the house. He never said a word.

I lay in bed listening to my mother ironing in the kitchen. I pictured her ironing. The hiss of steam. The sprinkle bottle she used to wet my Dad's shirts. I pictured her face staring down at the shirt as her arm moved back and forth in a steady tempo.

TASK

1 The story is written in a style which causes us to be very involved in it. Choose three moments which you consider to be important. Briefly describe them and explain your reactions to them.

2 The place names in this story are clearly American but there are a whole host of details which put this story clearly in its American setting and culture. Explain what, for you, gives the story its American feel.

TASK 3

You are sometimes given quite a lot of stimulus material and the first thing to do is to read it carefully. When examiners set a paper they consider the length of the stimulus material and make allowances for the time you will take to read it. So do not worry if you spend some time reading and thinking – you must do this before you start writing.

This question paper is based on newspaper articles about the problems which can be caused by difficult neighbours. Before you read them, look at the tasks you have to do at the end of the stimulus material. Think about these tasks as you read the articles. You may, if you wish, make notes alongside them and underline or highlight anything that helps you plan your answers.

STIMULUS MATERIAL

Spitting Distance
BRITAIN'S WORST NEIGHBOURS

If an Englishman's home is his castle, what happens when Mr and Mrs Genghis Khan move in next door? What about Miss Saturday Night Party, Mr Midnight Strimmer or Mrs That's My Parking Space? Or even Mr and Mrs Slightly Irritating But They Will Do It Again And Again?

Nobody would ever admit to being the neighbours from hell, but a lot of people think they're living next door to them (and often the feeling is mutual).

"The only way to describe it is torture," said Jean Hughes. So irritating was her experience with a Miss South-East London Ghetto Blaster that she set up the Right to Peace and Quiet Campaign. "Often when you complain, they realise they have got some power over you, the power to do it again. And then you end up living your life in constant fear of something happening."

The kind of fear that is the constant companion of the Thompson family, who live on a council estate. Sidney and his wife, Thelma, are both in their seventies and have lived in the same end-of-terrace house for 25 years. It was always an ordinary kind of place – respectable working-class, if you will – and full of the kind of noise and boisterousness you'd expect. But it was pleasant.

Until, that is, last November, when the Pope family moved in next door. That they had eight children was nothing out of the ordinary – the Thompsons had had nine. That they had Rottweilers... well, again, they're scarcely uncommon around there. But four of them?

The Popes quickly made their mark. Nothing spectacular, mind, just persistent noise, barrages of verbal abuse, daily fights among themselves, and a garden so full of dog excrement that the Thompsons called in an environmental health officer. The kind of things that, taken

5 Exam practice

in isolation, are no more than a nuisance – if they happen occasionally. But they happened round the clock, and, said Mr Thompson, "If you ask the Popes to be quiet, they just jeer and clap their hands." The family on the other side of the Popes, who had lived there for 16 years, moved away. Another neighbour, who refused to be identified, even went so far as to purchase an air pistol to protect herself, although a second liked the Popes so much that she has moved in with them.

Now the Popes, too, are finding themselves sinned against: their windows were mysteriously smashed one night earlier this month. Around the same time, encouraged by Pope children, the Pope dogs chased three children from open land. Baseball bats were waved. The police were called in the middle of the night.

Why had the Popes been moved there in the first place? "They were homeless and we had an obligation to rehouse them," said a council official earlier this year. And why were they homeless? Because their previous council house had burnt down. It took four fire teams to tackle the blaze. "I've never seen a house so damaged so quickly," said the fire chief at the time. And why did the Popes have to remain next door to the Thompsons? Because it was a condition of Mr and Mrs Pope's bail. And what were they out on bail for? Arson.

Not that such conflicts are the preserve of council estates. Them Next Door versus Us In Here is probably the reason laws were first laid down.

"Your next-door neighbour," wrote G K Chesterton more than 70 years ago, "is not a man; he is an environment. He is the barking of a dog; he is the noise of a pianola; he is a dispute about a party wall; he is drains that are worse than yours, or roses that are better than yours."

Listen to John McVicar, the journalist and, let's face it, former bank robber. Even he is not immune to the temptations of the neighbourhood watch-it. "A girl upstairs flooded my place with her washing machine and we had a big row about it."

Later, he had a run-in with another neighbour. "She tried to nick my parking place. So I blocked her off. She nipped out of her car, ran over and let my tyres down. So I let hers down."

If Jean Hughes was ever tempted to retaliate, she kept her counsel, but the road to her founding the Right to Peace and Quiet Campaign was a long and noisy one. Particularly, she will never forget her neighbour's favourite record, Lisa Stansfield's All Around The World. "I could hear it right through the wall just about every day – word for word for word. And it's not as if I didn't like Lisa Stansfield's music. I love listening to her, but when I choose to listen to her." As Hughes pointed out, loud music is a potent form of torture. When the Americans wanted to winkle out General Noriega, they bombarded him with festival-strength heavy rock.

Hughes found herself wondering about the psychology of such neighbours from hell. "People should look at it," she says. "Often it's to do with status. They feel they don't have it, and it's a way of getting back at the people next door. My neighbour was a single mother and probably felt jealous as I was buying my council house. Also, playing music at that level gives you a bit of a buzz, like going to a disco." Both she and her partner – her word – are DJs. "That buzz can be important for people who can't get out much. And it can be addictive."

The psychology of the next-door neighbour is something that has often crossed the mind of New Zealand-born dentist, David Benson. Some 17 years ago, he moved into a Wiltshire village. He has one big bugbear in his life, 10 years of disruption and confusion, occasioned, in the view of Benson and other people in the village, by his neighbour, the wife of the local vicar. As so often, when put down on paper, the details of the complaints look trivial, even silly. Apple bombardments, late-night lawn mowing and hedge trimming, a running row about the use of the lane for parking. Eventually, of course, it became something of a two-way thing. In some ways, the details are almost irrelevant. The point is that they went on and on, starting in 1984, and that other villagers also suffered abuse.

His wife, Sue, is more philosophical about it all, or maybe just more resigned. "It bothers

David more than me. It's intruding on his male territory. But if only the Church had come to us a couple of years ago and said, 'Please be patient'."

At this point it is worth mentioning that the teaching 'Love Your Neighbour' appears in many religions. We've all heard it. It's the doing of it that's just about impossible.

(Adapted from an article by Peter Silverton in *The Observer* ©)

Hate Thy Neighbour

STIMULUS MATERIAL

May 1993. Emma Greensmith, a grandmother, was found guilty of playing Jim Reeves records 18 hours a day. Her hi-fi was seized and visitors were barred from her house between the hours of 9pm and 9am.

November 1992. Nigel and Sonia Hicks were evicted after 14 months of an onslaught against their neighbours. They hopped along in front of a crippled war veteran, Jack Tilting, yelling abuse. They stuck a rude poster in their window, chopped wood and played loud music in the early hours. They were sent to separate hostels.

January 1990. John Eales became so fed up with his neighbour that he drilled holes in his floor and poured petrol through them to the flat below. He was given a conditional discharge.

June 1992. Donald Jeffers was arrested for his own safety and bound over for 18 months for his terrorising of his neighbour, Veronica Edwards. He'd complained her budgies were noisy and reported her to the RSPCA. He'd told her teenage son she was a witch, dumped grass cuttings over her fence and photographed her at the washing line.

April 1990. After blitzing neighbours for two years with junk mail, Tracey Davies was given a conditional discharge, and ordered to pay £10 costs and £50 compensation.

November 1991. Bert and Mary Stanley, both 75, banged on their ceiling if anyone walked on the floor above, hurled abuse at neighbours strolling in the street, called the police to a noisy party at which everyone was, in fact, asleep, and terrified a couple into watching TV with the sound off. The council offered 17 witnesses.

September 1991. In a dispute over a parking space, Joanne and Fred Cooper were alleged to have menaced the family of 'That's Life's' Howard Leader with lumps of wood, and threatened to shoot a neighbour's cat and nail it to the door if it came near their aviary.

5 Exam practice

STIMULUS MATERIAL

Battle lines: John Gladden's home improvements have left him at odds with his Norbury neighbours and his local council.

TASK

1   You have been asked to write the words for an information leaflet on behalf of the *Right to Peace and Quiet Campaign*. By referring to the article "Spitting Distance", the photograph and the material headed "Hate Thy Neighbour":

(a)   summarise the things people do which annoy and upset their neighbours.

(b)   explain the reasons given in the material for neighbours behaving so badly.   (20)

Write in paragraphs using your own words.
You should write about 200–250 words altogether.

2   How does the writer try to make "Spitting Distance" interesting and entertaining?
In your answer you should consider:

- the incidents and the characters he describes
- his choice of words in the article.   (20)

MEG 1995

62

Exam practice 5

This example is taken from the London Reading and Response Paper 1995.

A Very French Future

FUTUROSCOPE:
France's space-age theme park is lots of fun, even without any roller-coasters

I have seen the future and it works. It is called Futuroscope and it is France's own answer to Euro Disney.

While Mickey Mouse and his fellow American characters are to be found cuckoo-like near Paris, Futuroscope lies just outside Poitiers, 200 miles south of the capital. It makes a fascinating contrast to Euro Disney. The French love it. Attendances topped the two million mark last year for the first time since it opened in 1987. Until now, 93 per cent of visitors have been French; fewer than two per cent have come from Britain.

Can they hope to attract more of us? I took Daniel, my nine-year-old, along to test it from both child and adult viewpoints.

So keen are the French on very modern architecture that Futuroscope might be a new development in Paris: a series of space-age pavilions dotted around a pleasant park with plenty of lakes, fountains and flowers, divided by a walkway. It's very easy and not at all tiring to walk around, but expect queues of up to an hour outside some pavilions during high season.

Daniel was disappointed when I first broke the news to him that there were no roller-coasters, but he cheered up when we sampled the three "dynamic motion" simulators. The first put us in the cockpit of a bobsleigh descending a steep, twisting course like a Cresta Run. It was a totally realistic and terrifying five minutes. Daniel loved it. The second ride followed, almost as scary, on a runaway mine wagon …

The third simulator, which opened this spring, is the park's newest attraction. Shown on a massive screen, it was a combination of a film about the region and an exhilarating ride through it, finishing with a high-speed drive in a runaway racing car through the streets of Poitiers. Daniel judged it "the best so far", and preferred all the simulators to Euro Disney's outdoor rides which he thought were "too slow".

But he found even the simulators much less exciting than the two three-dimensional cinemas. Like many of Futuroscope's attractions, they are designed to educate as well as entertain. One explained the nature of molecules, the other was about an African safari, which featured a leopard apparently leaping straight out of the screen and into the audience. Daniel found this deeply satisfying. So did the hordes of French children who were swarming around the park in school parties. Unlike other theme parks I have visited, there were also many older visitors, who appeared to take great pride in it.

Futuroscope is worth a day of your holiday if you're anywhere near Poitiers this summer, and could even make a stimulating weekend excursion from Britain. There are several hotels near to the park, ranging from one to three stars.

Daniel's verdict was: "Can we come back again soon?"

TASK 4

STIMULUS MATERIAL

TASK

(a) This article is about an attraction on offer to holiday-makers in France, Futuroscope. What are the main attractions of Futuroscope? You should write your answer in about 100 words.

and

(b) Write a letter to the headteacher and governors at your school, to convince them that a school visit to **either** Euro Disney **or** Futuroscope would be a good idea. Explain what you think would make the visit a success.

Edexcel 1995

5 Exam practice

TASK 5

STIMULUS MATERIAL

Read the passage that follows. It is adapted from *The Pupil* by Caro Fraser, published by Phoenix (1993) and describes a London market in the present day.

Wednesday was not going well for Anthony Cross. His day had begun at 4 a.m., and it was now nearly nine. It had been drizzling steadily since the first grey shadows of dawn had crept over the city, and the lanes and alleyways around Spitalfields market were glistening with rain and vegetable refuse. The great steel barn of the fruit market echoed with the shouts of porters, the whinings of fork-lift trucks, the crashings of crates and the tramp of feet. Things were only just beginning to slacken off.

Anthony had a holiday job in the market as a porter. He worked for an importer called Amos Oxford, and was subject to the brute tyranny of Mr Mant, a lowly clerk in the employ of Mr Oxford. What Mr Mant did was not very clear, but it seemed that he had been doing it at Spitalfields, man and boy, for forty years. While Anthony hauled crates and tallied sacks of onions, Mr Mant would emerge regularly from the cracked wooden den that he called his office, and where he spent murmuring hours thumbing through dirty lists of produce, and shuffle across to the cafe with his little stainless steel teapot. There it would be filled, and Mr Mant, small and dark and bent and unwashed, would make his way back to his office with his tea and a doughnut. He never offered to share his tea with Anthony.

It was the mere fact of the steady rain that made Anthony's life so miserable. Wheeling the heavy handcart, with its iron-rimmed wheels, in and out of the market, he had become drenched. There was nothing waterproof he could wear without sweating horribly, and now he could feel the damp seeping in under his jersey, through his shirt and into his skin, blotting and chilling him. The rain made the cobbles slippery, and a treacherous film of muck and rotten vegetable matter lay everywhere. Anthony's working gloves had become sodden and unmanageably heavy, forcing him to discard them, and now his hands were chafed from tiny splinters on the sides of the raw wooden pallets. Dodging the roaring fork-lifts, he made his way to the cafe and bought his first cup of tea of the day. He leaned against a pillar of the market and gazed vacantly as he drank it, a tall, good-looking boy, with deep, thoughtful eyes, and dark hair matted with the rain. He stared unseeingly at the mountains of produce, at the piles of fat melons and bloom-covered purple grapes, at the light wooden boxes afloat with parsley, the gleaming green peppers, box upon box. The overhead lights gave everything an unreal lustre, like a great, bountiful harvest in a stone and iron setting.

Through the cockney clamour of the porters and traders, the sharp babble of voices rose and fell. Buyers of every race and description crowded the refuse-strewn lanes around the market with their vans and carts.

As Anthony watched it all, he saw out of the corner of his eye Mr Mant returning from the pub. With a sigh, he tossed his plastic cup among the rest of the rubbish and turned to his final, distasteful task of the morning, the disposal of five rotten bags of potatoes. Through the fibre of the sacking oozed liquefying potato, and the stench choked Anthony as he hauled the slimy sacks, dragging them across to the other piles of refuse near the car park, where the scavengers were already congregating.

As he pondered the dreadful possibility of spending one's entire life as a market porter, with the echoing sheds of Spitalfields forming the boundaries of one's vision, the very epitome of his musings suddenly turned the corner from a side street and came lurching towards him in a fork-lift truck driven at full speed. Len and he were friends, if only by reason of their proximity in age, but the differing scopes of their separate ambitions and dreams often formed part of Anthony's private meditations. Apart from a burning, but unrealised longing to play striker for Millwall Football Club, Len's great ambition in life, ever since he had first come to work at the market at the age of sixteen, had been to drive a fork-lift truck. It struck him as the height of sophistication to career around in a battered Toyota at speeds far greater than were strictly desirable or necessary, exchanging banter and obscenities with other drivers, forking up sheaves of pallets with utter disregard for the safety of their contents, and, of course, chain-smoking throughout the entire operation without ever seeming to move one's hands from the controls. Len had eventually

Exam practice 5

achieved his ambition at the age of twenty. Someone had once foolishly remarked in Len's hearing that it was particularly difficult to overturn a fork-lift truck; snatching up this gauntlet, Len had proceeded to overturn two Nissans and a Toyota within the space of three months, before receiving a severe warning from the supervisor.

That Wednesday, Anthony watched him as he sped through the rain, dropped down a gear, braked, and came to rest in a crate of lemons.

" 'Allo, Tone," he said nonchalantly. "Fancy some grub?"

Anthony's mouth watered at the thought of a mushroom omelette and fried bread, washed down by a large cup of hot, sweet coffee. He glanced round. Mr Mant had apparently gone back to converse with his circle of acquaintance in The Gun. He nodded, and they set off through the rain to the cafe.

Len was a tall, well-made youth of twenty-two, cheerful of disposition and, it must be said, fairly simple. He regarded Anthony with a mix of admiration (for his obvious intelligence) and pity (for his inability to appreciate the finer things in life, such as Millwall and Worthington Best Bitter). Their discussions were normally limited to cars and television programmes, but now and then Len's imagination would be fired by a leader in *The Sun*, and he would seek out Anthony to discuss current affairs with him, feeling that Anthony's views lent breadth to his own, and that he could safely rehearse those views to his own credit later in the pub.

Len had finished his mixed grill and was watching Anthony speculatively as he mopped up the last of his mushroom omelette.

" 'Ow long are you working 'ere, then, Tone?" He lit a cigarette, leaned his face on his hand, and stared deeply at Anthony. Anthony looked up.

"I don't know. Not much longer. Until I finish my apprenticeship for becoming a barrister."

Len's interest slipped away from Anthony and his career, and moved on to more immediate interests.

"You fancy coming to a disco in Hackney tonight?"

Anthony shook his head; he had never yet accepted one of Len's invitations, but he was touched that Len continued to issue them.

"I can't. I've got to go and see my father," he said. And then he sighed, thinking of his father and wishing that he could go to Hackney, after all.

Answer **all** the questions that follow.

1 For what reasons was Wednesday "not going well for Anthony Cross"?

2 What are you told about Len and what impression does the writer give of him?

3 What do you learn about the thoughts and feelings of Anthony Cross?

4 The writer is an observer of Spitalfields market and those who go there. Explain, with examples, how she uses words and phrases to bring the market to life.

SEG 1995

5 Exam practice

TASK 6

This 1995 paper gave a chance to do a variety of writing. First of all there is a picture and then there are three associated possible tasks. In this case each of the tasks requires a different style of writing. The first is a particularly personal piece of writing; the second gives you a chance to develop a story which needs an effective central character; the third is a piece of discursive writing where you are asked to develop an argument. You might like to practise by doing all three tasks and then deciding which task you felt you coped with best and was most satisfying.

STIMULUS MATERIAL

TASK

FIRST   **Look at the picture above.**
        It shows people in hospital during visiting time.
NEXT   Think about times you have been in hospitals as a patient, or a visitor.

WHAT YOU HAVE TO WRITE

1 **Describe** as vividly as you can

   either   (a)   an experience you have had as a hospital patient,
   or   (b)   an occasion when you visited someone in hospital.

   OR

2 **Write a short story** in which the main character is someone working in a hospital.

   OR

3 "Good health is the responsibility of the individual."
   Write your views on this statement.

SEB 1995

The passage describes an attack during the First World War.

The artillery barrage was due to start in fifteen minutes' time. Prior shared a bar of chocolate with Robson, sitting hunched up together against the cold damp mist. Then they started crawling forward. The Manchester Regiment had to advance over the waterlogged fields. The rain had stopped, but the already marshy ground had flooded in places, and over each
5 stretch of water lay a thick blanket of mist. Concentrate on nothing but the moment, Prior told himself, moving forward on knees and elbows like a frog or a lizard or like – like anything except a man. Even with all this mist there was now a perceptible thinning of the light, a gleam from the canal where it ran between spindly, dead trees.

  There is to be no retirement under any circumstances. That was the order. They have tied
10 us to the stake, Prior thought. We cannot fly, but bear-like we must fight the course. The men were silent, staring straight ahead into the mist. Talk, even in whispers, was forbidden. Prior looked at his watch, licked dry lips, watched the second hand crawl to the quarter hour. All around him was a tension of held breath. 5.43. Two more minutes. He crouched further down, whistle clenched between his teeth.

15   Prompt as ever, hell erupted. Shells whined over, flashes of light, plumes of water from the drainage ditches, tons of mud and earth flung into the air. A shell fell short. The ground shook beneath them and a shower of pebbles and clods of earth peppered their steel helmets. Five minutes of this, five minutes of the air bursting in waves against your face, men with dazed faces braced against it, as they picked up the light bridges meant for fording the
20 flooded drainage ditches, and carried them out to the front. Then, abruptly, silence. A gasp for air, then noise again, but further back, as the barrage lifted.

  Prior blew the whistle, couldn't hear it, was on his feet and running anyway, urging the men on with wordless cries. They rushed forward, making for the line of trees. Prior kept shouting, 'Steady, steady! Not too fast on the left!' It was important there should be no
25 bunching when they reached the bridges. The men were stumbling into quagmires or tripping over clumps of grass. A shell whizzing over from the German side exploded in a shower of mud and water. He saw several little figures topple over, it didn't look serious, somehow, they didn't look like beings who could be hurt.

  The bridges were laid down, quickly, efficiently, no bunching at the crossings, just the
30 clump of boots on wood, and then they emerged from beneath the shelter of the trees and out into the terrifying openness of the bank. As bare as an eyeball, no cover anywhere, and the machine gunners on the other side were alive and well. They dropped down, firing to cover the engineers as they struggled to assemble the bridge, but nothing covered them. Bullets fell like rain and the men started to fall. Prior saw the man next to him, a silent,
35 surprised face as he twirled and fell, a slash of scarlet like a huge flower bursting open on his chest. Crawling forward, he fired at the bank opposite though he could hardly see it for the clouds of smoke that drifted across. Only two engineers were left, still struggling with the bridge. And still the terrible rain fell. Kirk paddled out in a crate to give covering fire, was hit, hit again, this time in the face, went on firing directly at the machine gunners who
40 crouched in their defended holes only a few yards away. Prior was about to start across the water with ammunition when he was hit, though it didn't feel like a bullet, more like a blow from a truncheon or a cricket bat, only it knocked him off his feet and he fell, one arm trailing over the edge of the canal.

  He tried to turn to crawl back beyond the drainage ditches, knowing that it was only a
45 matter of time before he was hit again. Simple repetitive thoughts ran round and round his brain. *What a mess. What a shambles. Madness.* There was no pain, more a spreading numbness that left his brain clear. He saw Kirk die. He saw Owen die, his body lifted off the ground by bullets, describing a slow arc in the air as it fell. It seemed to take for ever to fall,

5 Exam practice

and Prior's consciousness fluttered down with it. He gazed at his reflection in the water,
50 which broke and reformed and broke again as bullets hit the surface and then, gradually, as
the numbness spread, he ceased to see it.

* * * * *

On the edge of the canal the Manchesters lie. The stretcher-bearers have departed with the
last of the wounded and the dead are left alone. The battle has withdrawn from them; the
bridge they succeeded in building was destroyed by a single shell.

55 The sun has risen. The first shaft strikes the water and creeps towards them along the bank,
finding here the back of a hand, there the side of a neck, lending a rosy glow to skin from
which the blood has fled, and then, finding nothing here that can respond to it, the shaft of
light passes over them and begins to probe the distant fields.

(Adapted from 'The Ghost Road' by Pat Barker)

TASK

1 **Look again at lines 1–14.**
What thoughts and feelings do Prior and his men experience as they wait for the moment to attack?
Your answer should be based on close reference to the text. (10)

2 **Look again at lines 15–51.**
How does the writer convey the horror of the attack on the canal? (10)

3 **Look again at lines 52–58.**
How effective do you find these lines as an ending to the passage as a whole?
Think about:
- the feelings you experience as you read these lines;
- the mood and atmosphere;
- the writer's technique and use of language. (10)

WJEC 1998

Exam practice 5

*Answer **all** the following questions.*

TASK 8

The **Resource Material** on pages 71 and 72 comes from a booklet advertising holidays in the Llandudno area.

The passage overleaf (**A View of Llandudno**) has been adapted from a book of travel writing by Bill Bryson, an American who has lived in Britain for many years.

1   Look at the advertisement *Where Memories are made of SEA, SAND and FUN*.
    What different groups of people is this advertisement trying to attract to Llandudno?
    How does it try to appeal to each group?
    Think about the text and the pictures. (10)

2   Look at lines 7–24 of *A View of Llandudno*.
    Bill Bryson clearly hates the guesthouse in Llandudno in which he stayed.
    How does he convey his feelings to you?
    In your answer comment on:
    • his use of fact and opinion;
    • his choice of language;
    • the way he creates mood and atmosphere.

3   Now consider the whole passage, *A View of Llandudno*.
    What are Bill Bryson's attitudes to the holiday resort of Llandudno as a whole?
    How does he convey his attitudes?
    Think about what he says and how he says it.

4   **Consider both the advertisement *and* the passage.**
    The images of Llandudno presented in these two texts are very different.
    In what ways are they different?
    Refer to details in the advertisement and the passage to support your answer. (10)

5 Exam practice

STIMULUS MATERIAL

A View of Llandudno

Llandudno is truly a fine and handsome place, built on a generously proportioned bay and lined along its front with a huddle of prim but gracious nineteenth-century hotels. It was built as a holiday resort in the mid-1800s and it cultivates a nice old-fashioned air.

When I arrived, I discovered that the town was packed with weekending pensioners. Coaches from all over were parked along the side-streets. Every hotel I called at was full and in every dining room I could see crowds of nodding white heads spooning soup and conversing happily.

Further along the front there stood a clutch of guesthouses and a few of them had vacancy signs perched in their windows. I selected a place that looked reasonable enough from the outside – it promised colour TV and coffee-making facilities, about all I require these days for a lively
10 Saturday night – but from the moment I set foot in the door and drew in the mildewy smell of damp plaster and peeling wallpaper, I knew it was a bad choice. I was about to flee when the proprietor appeared and revealed that a single room with breakfast could be had for £19.50 – little short of a swindle. It was entirely out of the question that I would stay the night in such a dismal place at such an extortionate price, so I said, 'That sounds fine,' and signed in. Well, it's so hard to
15 say no.

My room was everything I expected it to be – cold and cheerless, with ugly furniture, grubbily matted carpet and those mysterious ceiling stains that bring to mind a neglected corpse in the room above. Fingers of icy wind slipped through the single, ill-fitting window. The curtains had to be yanked violently before they would budge and came nowhere near meeting in the middle. There
20 was a tray of coffee things but the cups were disgusting and the spoon was stuck to the tray. The bathroom, faintly illuminated by a distant light activated by a length of string, had curling floor tiles and years of accumulated muck packed into every corner and crevice. A bath was out of the question, so I threw some cold water on my face, dried it with a towel that had the texture of a Weetabix and gladly went out.

25 I had a long stroll along the prom to boost my appetite and pass an hour. It felt wonderful. The air was still and sharp and there wasn't a soul about, though there were still lots of white heads in the hotel lounges, all bobbing merrily about. I walked nearly the length of The Parade, enjoying the chill autumn air and the trim handsomeness of the setting: a soft glow of hotels to the left and an inky void of restless sea to my right.

30 I dined simply in a small, nondescript restaurant and afterwards set off to hunt for a pub. Llandudno had surprisingly few of these vital institutions. I walked for some time before I found one that looked even vaguely approachable. It was a typical town pub inside – stale, smoky, noisy and busy. I sat at the bar for a while and, as sometimes happens in these circumstances, I had a sudden urge to return to my seafront lodgings for an early night.

35 In the morning, I emerged from the guesthouse into a world drained of colour. The sky was low and heavy and the sea vast, lifeless and grey. As I walked along, rain began to fall.

(Adapted from 'Notes from a Small Island' by Bill Bryson)

Exam practice 5

where
memories
are made of
**SEA, SAND
& FUN**

Letts
Q&A

5 Exam practice

No childhood is quite complete without remembered dreams of halcyon days spent at the seaside, paddling in the waters or playing on the sands.

Llandudno has two beaches on either side of the town. The quieter West Shore with its long sandy beach and children's play area has wonderful views of the Conwy Estuary, Isle of Anglesey and Puffin Island, site of a Cistercian monastery.

North Shore is the lively beach, spanning the two mile crescent bay for which Llandudno is famed.

Its popularity has stood the test of time. The traditional still thrives in the form of Punch and Judy shows, donkey rides and organised games. On the Pier there are stalls and amusements including Professor Peabody's Playplace with supervised activities for children. On the opposite end of the promenade, at Craig-y-Don, toddlers love splashing about in the paddling pool.

The Promenade itself is a hive of activity during the glorious months of summer. There are fun events such as the charity pram race and bed making competitions. The waiter and waitress race, a keenly fought title by the town's hotels, is in its 26th year. On balmy summer evenings listen to the sounds of local or visiting bands on the bandstand.

For fun and frivolity, sunbathing and people-watching, Llandudno is truly the place where memories are made.

Neighbouring Llanfairfechan, a small coastal resort town, is an excellent starting point for energetic walks as it is surrounded by woodlands, mountain scenery and seascapes. There's a long safe open stretch of sand and visiting yachtsmen are welcome at the Sailing Club. There are opportunities for angling, riding, windsurfing or to play a round of golf on the town's nine hole course.

Llandudno North Shore and Llanfairfechan are Tidy Britain Seaside Award Winners.

AT A GLANCE

Angling
Sea fishing from the pier all year round. Day tickets available at the pier. Tel: (01492) 876258.

Bait
Available from Kiosk by the Pier or from "Llandudno Fishing Tackle", Craig-y-Don. Tel: (01492) 878425.

Boat Trips
Half hour trips around Great Orme's Head depart frequently from the jetty, North Shore Promenade, May-September. Tel. (01492) 877394

Fishing Trips
Organised by boatmen at Conwy and Llandudno. Contact the Harbour Master for further details. Tel: (01492) 596253

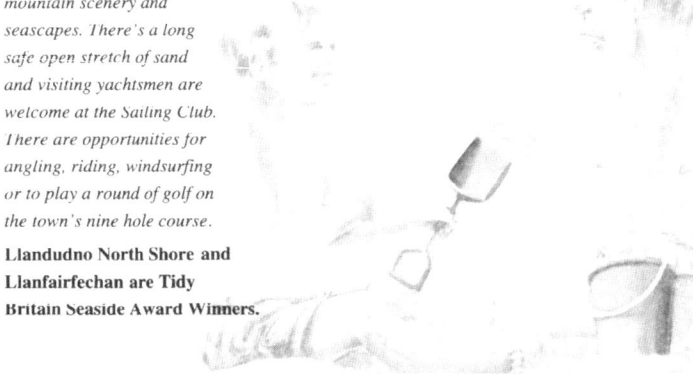

WJEC 1998

Exam practice 5

The pages which follow provide advice, in the form of examiner's tips, on how to tackle the tasks set in this exam practice section. Read the general points first before turning to the more specific advice given for each particular task.

EXAMINER'S TIPS

General points
On the front of examination papers there is always a certain amount of rubric (advice for you to follow). Always make sure that you read and follow the rubric. Below is a good example:

Pay close attention to what you are asked to write.
PLAN what you are going to write.
Read and check your work before you hand it in.
Any changes to your work should be made clearly.

- Remember that it is a National Curriculum requirement that within any mark scheme there must be separate marks awarded for spelling, handwriting and presentation, so be very attentive to these features of your writing.

- When you are thinking through and preparing your answers do not be afraid to underline and make notes on the examination paper. You may choose to use highlighter pens. What is important is that you think your way through any task before starting to write your answer.

- Make sure that, whatever the task, you include those elements in your writing which distinguish between the pedestrian and the really good – variety of sentence structure including the use of complex sentences, sophisticated vocabulary, perhaps dialogue (correctly punctuated and paragraphed) and so on.

- Look for the number of marks available for a question or task. This is the important sort of clue that you should look for in any examination in any subject. This information will give you a fairly clear idea of the relative difficulty of questions, of the amount of time you should spend on each question and so on.

Task	Examiner's tips
1	• You will probably consider that the teacher is, in fact, very rude, offhand and dismissive. You might even suggest that the teacher is jealous or intimidated which would be a very interesting point. Why do you think the teacher invited the poet in the first place?
	• There is also a very solid answer to the second part of the Question 1. The examples are well picked out and the reactions to the points are very sensible, clear and justifiable.
	• The third part of Question 1 is rather more difficult. It is right to pick out the references to assonance and rhyme; some of you would have been able to pick up the quotation on Keats and might have had some idea of the sort of poetry written by Kipling. In showing the attitude of the teacher the word "sadly" might well have been picked out also.
	• Before launching into an answer to Question 2 thought should be given both to what you as the poet really thought about the way you were treated and also about who you were speaking to: mother; husband; wife; child, etc. Your decisions would then determine your approach to the writing. Quite often there is a second part to an examination paper which asks for a piece of writing with the expectation being at least a side as an answer.

5 Exam practice

Task	Examiner's tips
2	• There are two tasks here arising from the excerpt from "Motel Chronicles"; the first task is distinctly more straightforward than the second. You are free to choose from the extract any moment which might be considered significant provided that you can give an explanation for your choice. You might, for instance, pick the moment when the boys arrive at the mouth of the tunnel, or the very end of the story when the boy is whipped by his father.
	• The second task is rather more difficult and goes right to the heart of "writing from other cultures". You might have a particular and personal perception of American life which you could pursue. Whether or not it is a particularly "correct" or good view is something for you to think about yourself. Certainly you should write carefully about Americanisms in the language and make references to the natural life of the United States. When you are planning an answer for this task it might be an idea to go through the extract marking all the Americanisms and clearly American references. The first reference would be Juvenile Hall; you would pick out words like "creek"; and you would need to understand, "We caught Crawdads with marshmallow bait then tore the shells off them and used their meat to catch more Crawdads"; and so on.
	• Key words in the Question 2 are "culture" and "setting" and you should make sure that you deal with both in your answer.
3	• Make sure that you have read all the stimulus material and have used it.
	• First of all, this question gives you a context for your writing in that you are asked to provide the text for an information leaflet. If you continue that idea you are then given the ideas for two paragraphs which your text will sensibly contain. There is only a limited space and so you have been given a word length to work to. What you must do therefore is summarise the information.
	• Question 2 asks you to reflect on the main article which has been used as stimulus material. You are asked to consider how and why it is interesting and entertaining. You are then pointed to incidents, characters and the writer's use of language. Make sure in your answer you have covered all three of these areas, perhaps especially the writer's use of words.
4	• There are two tasks. The first is fairly straightforward. It is asking you to extract information from the passage and to express that information succinctly. It is asking for about 100 words and, although this is giving you some leeway, you should aim at between 90 and 110 words. They should also be your own words. Don't be content with your first draft but revise it to make sure that you are expressing the information in the best possible way. Don't be satisfied even if your first draft is a perfect length.
	• The second task is asking you to write a formal letter, so make sure that the language is appropriate, Remember to get the tone right, after all you want the headteacher and governors to agree with you that the visit would be a good idea. Remember also that they are likely to be more sympathetic if you can find an educational basis for the visit rather than just a fun basis. Your letter should be well set out and neat on the page

Exam practice 5

Task	Examiner's tips
5	• The tasks are based on a fairly lengthy narrative passage which is quite straightforward but which nevertheless needs to be read carefully several times. • You are not being asked just for the story but you are being asked to analyse character and to examine the language being used. All four questions had the same allocation of marks when the question was set. • Make sure that your answers are succinct and clear and that you do not waffle. Distinguish the characters carefully and make sure you explain your choice of phrases. There are not right and wrong answers; you might like "great, bountiful harvest in a stone and iron setting" or "oozed liquefying potato" which are good contrasts, but then you might prefer others.
6	• Remember that no one sort of writing is any more worthy than another. If you are given a choice, as you are here, it is a genuine choice. So if you know that you are better writing discursively than you are imaginatively, or vice versa, then choose the type of writing which you prefer. • Question 1 requires personal writing. A good answer will explore as well as describe a personal experience. For Question 2, the story will need characterisation and settings. Try to avoid stereotypes of characters, and remember there are many possible characters to choose amongst. Question 3 requires a discussion or argument in your writing. You will need to plan your points carefully, perhaps presenting a balanced set of views. The style will probably be more formal.

7	• The questions here take you carefully through the passage and so there can be no excuses for irrelevance:
	  – read the passage carefully and probably several times;
	  – consider carefully the characters, Prior and his men;
	  – look carefully at the questions and mark the sections of the passage each of them deals with;
	  – the marks in brackets at the end of each question tell you that the same number of marks are available for each – this should be reflected in the substance of your answers.
	
	• As well as the basic questions, note the sentence in the first question, 'Your answer should be based on close reference to the text,' and the bullets in question 3 which take you through the question.
	
	• This is from a section of an examination paper which tests reading, which means that the marks are given for demonstrating a clear understanding of what has to be read. This does not, of course, mean that you should not bother about the quality of your writing or presentation, but it does mean that you should refer clearly to what you have read.

5 Exam practice

Task	Examiner's tips
8	• Make sure that you have read all the material and have used it.
	• Note that the questions are all worth the same number of marks and your answers should reflect this. The questions constantly remind you that your answers should be fully based on the material. Note carefully the bullets in Question 2 and the final sentences of each of the other questions.
	• Question 1 — This question is specifically directing you to the advertisement. You must look at the content, the style of the text and the pictures to help you form your opinion.
	• Question 2 — This question is really about the style of the writing and this is not the easiest thing to write about. Look carefully at the bullets, they are there to help you to think your way systematically through.
	• Question 3 — The key words in this question are 'what' and 'how'. Writing about the attitude which is shown by a writer is not easy but these two words will help you.
	• Question 4 — This last question is asking you to manipulate the material from both sources. Make sure that, in your answer, you refer to both more or less equally.

Mock examination paper 5

SAMPLE EXAMINATION PAPER

*Have a go at this mock up of an examination paper. It is unlikely to fit the format of your examination precisely as the boards are all different, but it incorporates a number of useful features. Try to complete it in one sitting of **two hours**. When you have done so, compare your work with the sample answers given on pages 82–84.*

ENGLISH PAPER
PART ONE

Printed on the following pages are two passages.

The first tells part of the story of a working nun, Sister Prejean. The second is an article about counselling.

Read both passages and do both questions 1 and 2 which follow.

Mock examination paper

A DAY IN THE LIFE OF SISTER PREJEAN

Sister Helen Prejean, 58, one of the sisters of St Joseph of Medaille, Louisiana, is a lifelong campaigner for the abolition of capital punishment. She has acted as spiritual adviser to several inmates of America's death row. Her book Dead Man Walking *was nominated for a Pulitzer prize and was made into a successful film by Tim Robbins.*

For six years I lived with my friend Sister Christopher. She died recently from breast cancer and I'm still living in her house. All through the night I listen for her voice and I wake thinking of her. She was my greatest friend in the world for over thirty years and it's as if I'd undergone an amputation.

I begin every day with prayer, which I believe is about listening, rather than hurling petitions. When Chris first died she felt very close, but now she's fading from me and I've had to change my whole method of communication. The other day I found the scarf she used to wear when all her hair fell out after chemo.

I joined the Sisters of St. Joseph when I was 18. It took me a while to realise the tremendous freedom it's given me; just to be able to write is such a joy. Every year you make a budget of what you need and then you share with the group all that you make. Because of the book and the film it's a hefty amount now, but before all that happened I was working among poor people on a stipend of $3000 a year.

I have a hermitage built into the garage and I head out there to be alone and to write. It also has my artwork in it, my clarinet and my exercise machine. I'll memorise poetry while I'm exercising; there's a great connection between learning something by heart and moving your muscles and sinews.

The phone and the fax never stop and I get letters the whole time from people asking me to speak or to help. I also travel a lot, talking and praying with victims' families. There's one law for the rich and one for the poor in this country: "If you ain't got the capital you get the punishment," the saying goes. You can be sure there are no rich people on death row. There are so many problems with the criminal justice system; if you don't have a deep spirituality sustaining you, you don't last long. You light your little flare and then you disappear.

I'm on my fifth death row prisoner now. Three have been executed, one got life and right now I'm visiting Dobie Williams in Louisiana State Penitentiary. He's a 33-year-old mentally retarded black man, convicted by an all-white jury of the murder of a white woman, and I think he may be innocent. We have open visits now and he makes me hug him three times, because to be touched in that environment is so powerful. I describe to him what's going on outside and talk about my experiences. He's stuck in this tiny cell 23 hours a day. I'm the whole world coming in.

I feel horror and rage and revulsion like everybody else. And confusion. When Chris was ill, she had to have a chest drain put into her lung. I could hear her screams down the hall and all I could think of was Faith Hathaway who was stabbed 17 times by Robert Lee Willie. But I'm like a boat on a current – I watched Robert Lee Willie die in the electric chair, and all he was was this tough little boy child who never had a chance.

I worked very closely with Tim on the film and we're still good friends. Every major Hollywood studio had turned the script down. The nun didn't fall in love and elope with the death row inmate: he was guilty of an appalling crime and he died. Nobody could see how it could work.

I learnt to cook while I was writing Dead Man Walking. It was so good to go into the kitchen and cut up celery at the end of the day. I like substantial food and I have a hearty appetite. I make calls and write until around 5pm, but after that I don't want to speak or take care of anyone: I just want to be deliciously alone.

Adapted from *The Sunday Times Magazine*, 28 September 1997

Counselling 'does more harm than good'

By David Fletcher, Health Correspondent

PROFESSIONAL counselling is largely a waste of time and does more to boost the ego of the counsellor than to help the victim, a leading trauma expert said yesterday.

Prof Yvonne McEwan said the booming profession was at best useless and at worst highly destructive to victims seeking help.

She accused professional counsellors of creating a nation of victims in order to boost their flagging careers in the medical profession.

"Counselling is ethically bankrupt and is practised by over-zealous, ignorant people who are feeding their own egos," she said. "The rights of the victims are being sacrificed to keep counsellors in jobs."

Prof McEwan, of Fife University, who advised the US government after the Oklahoma City bombing, launched her attack at a European trauma conference in London organised by London Transport.

"What makes and creates mental illness is the very system designed to help it," she added. "The legal profession and medicine have colluded in the whole fabrication of people undergoing trauma.

"By medicalising what is a non-medical condition and introducing a therapy subject matter that is vastly under-researched, over-used and vastly abused, medicine is propping up a lot of dwindling careers.

"The very people they are trying to help are being labelled by them, stigmatised with problems, and at the end of that they have problems with job promotion, getting mortgages and custody of children."

Prof McEwan, who has worked with victims of terrorism in Northern Ireland, also attacked the lack of control or regulation over counselling, pointing out that anyone can set up as a counsellor simply by putting a sign in their window. There are 30,000 in London alone.

"The whole disaster scene has become a growth industry since the Bradford fire. In Dunblane, for instance, there were far more counsellors than victims."

Dr Lorie Bisbey, a trauma expert for London Transport, called for mandatory licensing to help people wishing to see counsellors.

Counselling was defended by John Parker, of the Centre for Crisis Psychology.

"Many people need to speak to someone who is not part of their problem, often outside the family, and in some circumstances only a trained counsellor can do that job," he said.

He admitted, however, that there were charlatans and advised anyone seeking a counsellor to check whether they were registered with reputable bodies such as the British Association for Counselling or the British Psychological Association.

The Daily Telegraph, 27 September 1997

5 Mock examination paper

1 Use both passages and summarise what we learn for and against counselling from them.

Your summary must be in you own words, written in sentences, and should be about 150 words long.

20 marks

2 Sister Prejean and Professor Yvonne McEwan meet when they are both invited as guests on a radio phone-in show. As well as talking generally about their work they are able to talk about a specific case because Sister Prejean is counselling a prisoner on Death Row while Professor McEwan is counselling the family of his victim.

Write an extract of the conversation, during which the presenter interrupts them with several listeners' questions.

Your extract should be about a side and a half long.

20 marks

Mock examination paper 5

PART TWO

Choose one of the titles below and write a composition of about 400 words.

3 "I felt like a prisoner in my own home."

Write the story of the person who said that.

20 marks

4 The young man in the picture is looking very thoughtful.

Write about him in any way you like.

20 marks

5 Some people are very grateful for help; others don't want to be helped at all.

Do you think this is true and why should it be so?

20 marks

5 Mock examination paper

> **Examiner's tip** In the book you have been given chances to summarise, which is a very important skill. In the first question in Part One of the paper you have been asked not only to summarise but to put together material from two sources. Make sure that you have used both passages. There are about twenty different points which could be made, so check though to see how many you have made.
>
> In the second task there are three characters who speak. Two of them are distinct characters from the passages, one you have to invent. Make sure your invention has real character. Make sure that the conversation is set out neatly. The most obvious way to have set it out is as a play script, but you might have chosen to write it as direct speech.
>
> In Part Two of the paper you have been asked to write a piece of continuous prose. The first two tasks invite a story while the third invites a more discursive approach. Make sure that the style is right.
>
> To get a really good grade on a paper like this you will be expected to get well over 40 marks out of 60.

ANSWERS

PART 1

1

> *The counselling which Sister Prejean does is of a particular type. She is described as a spiritual adviser. She has spent her life working among poor people who have needed advice and help. Her counselling involves talking and praying. She believes that she helps the prisoners by talking about herself. She becomes very close to the prisoners by hugging them, but in another way she knows that she mustn't get too close. She thinks she is doing good.*
>
> *Other people who do counselling really don't know what they are doing and they are more interested in their own jobs than they are in the people they should be helping. A lot of the time they make the situation worse. There is no control over people who become counsellors, anyone can do it. The only way for counselling to be any good is if people are trained to do it.*

> **Examiner's commentary** This is an adequate answer. It is 149 words long, the precise length which is asked for in the question. The answer goes through each of the passages picking out relevant points but has made no attempt to put the ideas together. The assumption has been that the first passage is in favour of counselling while the second passage is against it and this is not entirely true as the second passage tries to analyse rather more while the first passage is a narrative. Because of the way the question has been approached, this answer is very close to lifting phrases unnecessarily from the passages.

2

Presenter: Hallo there! We are very pleased to have with us today, Sister Prejean, a sister from the St Joseph of Medaille group and Professor Yvonne McEwan, who is an expert in the field of counselling. Welcome ladies. Sister Prejean I have a question here for you. Our listener wants to know whether you are ever scared when you are visiting the inmates of Death Row.

Sister Prejean: No, I don't feel afraid because, to begin with at least, there are people with me, the guards, who would be ready to act quickly if anything went wrong. The prisoners are usually so grateful that someone has come to see them they just sit quietly and want to talk.

Professor Yvonne: That's all very well but what do you talk about? Those men are guilty and deserve to be punished. Do you think that anyone has to worry about them? Now I am seeing the family of one of their victims and they are having a dreadful time getting over the shock. The trouble is that do-gooders like you get it wrong and make things worse for people like the families.

Presenter: I have another question from one of our listeners. It is really for you, Professor Yvonne. This listener believes that they are very good at listening to people and helping them. They don't do it professionally at the moment but want to know how to get the training that you mentioned in your article.

Professor Yvonne: The first thing is that, just because you think you are good at helping people doesn't mean that you really are. You might be doing more harm than good. This is the trouble, but if you really want to train you should get in touch with the British Association for Counselling and they will tell you where you can go on a course. A good course will only cost you about a thousand pounds.

Sister Prejean: I believe that some people are very good listeners and will be helpful. You see, in a way, I don't give advice. I don't know if my prisoners are really guilty but their lawyers are the ones to see to that, not me. All I know is that my prisoners are waiting to die and I can try to show them the love of God. I don't think I'm a do-gooder, I'm just doing my job as a nun.

Professor Yvonne: I just get so angry when people make things worse for other people because they are so ignorant. It took me a very long time to become an expert and people seem to think that they are experts overnight.

Presenter: Thank you both for your time.

5 Mock examination paper

Examiner's commentary This is quite a good answer. Most importantly each of the speakers is given a good paragraph. Poor answers to this type of question have the speakers saying one line each at a time; this means that no ideas are properly developed. Each of the speakers here is reasonably well in role. The presenter simply asks the questions and doesn't interfere, which is good; Sister Prejean is quiet and calm which is again good because that is how you feel a nun would be; Professor Yvonne never really becomes abusive, but her frustration is shown. What the answer does not exploit is the hint given in the question that Sister Prejean is counselling a prisoner on Death Row while Professor Yvonne is counselling the family of the victim. This might have given a chance to explore what each of them was saying to the people they were counselling. The length is just about adequate. The structure and language are good.

PART 2

Examiner's commentary You are given three possibilities here for your personal writing. We have not produced a model answer because there are so many possibilities. They offer opportunities to write in a variety of ways. For instance, you might choose to approach Question 3 in a purely imaginative way, writing your own story but you might also choose to write seriously and informatively, using a real person as the basis for your writing. Question 4, using the photograph, is asking for your own imaginative narrative. Question 5 is asking for informative and analytical writing and, importantly, is asking you to express a view. Whichever title you choose, and whichever approach you use, it is important that you write in the right style for your purpose. Look back at the earlier sections of this book which deal with different styles of writing to remind yourself.

Remember, as always, the quality of what you write is more important than the length. In your time planning leave yourself an opportunity to check through what you have written.